D1528406

Preaching The Parables

Series IV, Cycle A

I Love To Tell The Story

Richard Louie Sheffield

CSS Publishing Company, Inc., Lima, Ohio

Unless otherwise marked, scripture quotations are taken from the *New Revised Standard Version of the Bible*, copyright 1989 by the Division of Christian Education of the National Council of the Churches of Christ in the USA. Used by permission.

Scripture quotations marked (NIV) are taken from the Holy Bible, New International Version. Copyright © 1973, 1978, 1984 International Bible Society. Used by permission of Zondervan Bible Publishers. All rights reserved.

Scripture quotations marked (CEV) are taken from the Holy Bible, the Contemporary English Version. Copyright © The American Bible Society 1995. Used by permission.

Scripture quotations marked (KJV) are taken from the King James Version of the Bible, in the public domain.

Scripture quotations marked (The Message) are from *The Message* by Eugene H. Peterson, copyright © 1993, 1994, 1995, 1996, 2000, 2001, 2002. Used by permission of NavPress Publishing Group. All rights reserved.

For more information about CSS Publishing Company resources, visit our website at www.csspub.com or e-mail us at custserv@csspub.com or call (800) 241-4056.

Cover by Barbara Spencer

ISSN: 1938-5579

ISBN-13: 978-0-7880-2458-0
ISBN-10: 0-7880-2458-2

PRINTED IN USA.

For
Bill and Jan

I Love To Tell The Story

I love to tell the story of unseen things above,
Of Jesus and His glory, of Jesus and His love.
I love to tell the story, because I know 'tis true;
It satisfies my longings as nothing else can do.

Refrain
I love to tell the story, 'twill be my theme in glory,
To tell the old, old story of Jesus and His love.

I love to tell the story; more wonderful it seems
Than all the golden fancies of all our golden dreams.
I love to tell the story, it did so much for me;
And that is just the reason I tell it now to thee.

Refrain

I love to tell the story; 'tis pleasant to repeat
What seems, each time I tell it, more wonderfully sweet.
I love to tell the story, for some have never heard
The message of salvation from God's own holy Word.

Refrain

I love to tell the story, for those who know it best
Seem hungering and thirsting to hear it like the rest.
And when, in scenes of glory, I sing the new, new song,
'Twill be the old, old story that I have loved so long.

Refrain

"I Love To Tell The Story," words by A. Katherine Hankey 1866; music by William G. Fischer, in *Joyful Songs*, Nos. 1 to 3 (Philadelphia, Pennsylvania: Methodist Episcopal Book Room, 1869).

Table Of Contents

Preface

In liturgical use the "Preface" is that part of what we Presbyterians call "The Great Thanksgiving" which precedes the *Sanctus* in what is commonly called "the communion prayer." It is the beginning of our giving thanks to God in the context of sharing bread and wine in communion with God in Christ and with each other.

The simple dictionary definition, and the usage here, is more mundane. "Preface" is synonymous with "introduction" and is basically an author's preliminary remarks. This is my "Preface" except I have preceded it with two things from my past that are very present with me now: old friends, Bill and Jan, and an older hymn, "I Love To Tell The Story."

Bill and Jan Murphey, to whom this book is dedicated, have been my friends, have mentored me, and have loved me for nearly thirty years. Bill was the pastor at the Jenkintown Presbyterian Church in Philadelphia when I was a student at Princeton Seminary. We worked together for two years and I was accorded the honor of becoming one of a small group of students known as "Murph's boys." (One of the "boys" is a woman, but that's another story!) Everyone assumed it meant "Bill's boys," but years of friendship have proved otherwise. "Murph" is really Bill *and* Jan. More than once I've unsettled the peace of "Murph-ease" — their home in retirement — with one crisis or another. I have been heard and helped and welcomed into their home. I am eternally grateful.

The hymn, "I Love To Tell The Story," goes back to my childhood. I grew up hearing it sung by people whose story was often one of need and hardship. I never forgot it, but also never dreamed I would grow up to do it. I sat in the pew in my childhood church week after week, sometimes using a stubby pencil to "fill in" all the little circles on the lines in the hymnbook, and listened to Mama and Daddy sing this hymn. If nothing else, it taught me that in the long run, whatever the preacher says, it's the hymns that will be remembered. It's in humble (if not completely willing) acceptance of that reality that I have preached the sermons in this book.

These particular sermons are all based on parables — stories Jesus told to incarnate the kingdom. Much as *he* brought us face to face with God, Jesus' *stories* bring us face to face with life as it is and as it will be; with what we might expect when "Thy kingdom come, Thy will be done, *on earth as it is in heaven*," is "answered prayer."

What I've discovered over the 25 years that have passed since those first years with "Murph" is that I really do "love to tell the story" — even on those days when I'm not sure I love everyone I'm telling it to. The story of "unseen things above" is how I make sense of what I see too well in the world around me. There was a time when I would have labeled this hymn "escapist," but now I see it as simply reassuring. It's a way, for me at least, to reach back to my roots and understand my call.

A decade ago CSS Publishing asked me to write another book of sermons. Then and now they have been most gracious in agreeing to publish them as they were preached. They have minimal alterations to remove personal or contemporary references. They are not generic, and no one, not even me, could carry them into a pulpit next Sunday and preach them as is. I hope that the way I have tried to "tell the story" is true to the stories Jesus told, called parables, and would be pleased and flattered if these sermons help others hear or tell the story themselves.

But why a book of sermons? Why not a book "about" parables? The simple answer is "because parables are sermons preached as stories." There is a place for "about" books and there are many available. CSS has a number of them in its catalog. If you want to read the classics I commend anything by Joachim Jeremias, C. H. Dodd, or William Barclay. There is a greater element of "teaching" in these sermons than I regularly do. The reason for that will become clear in the reading — Jesus was contemporary, too! We don't often find ourselves in *exactly* the same situation as do the people in his stories. That means we need a bit of help to find ourselves in the story at all. I've tried to "tell the story" with sidebars along the way to help the hearer hear the story as Jesus intended it. And I've avoided, as best I can, telling it "my way." The power of these stories is in their ability to let us hear Jesus. Sometimes, as I note in one of the sermons to follow, the best thing the preacher can do is get out of the way. I've tried.

It has struck me, though, in writing these over the past year, that Jesus was on to something. People not only love to tell stories, they love to hear them. Better yet, they remember them. Telling a story is a good way for a preacher to compete with the hymns! I've included lots of my own stories and some borrowed stories in these sermons, not as filler, but as ways of looking at Jesus' stories from different perspectives. I've tried to challenge myself, and I hope something I've said will challenge you as well. At least I hope what I've done hasn't gotten in the way of what Jesus was doing – reminding us "every-which-way" (as my grandma said), that God is on our side; God loves us; and nothing in this life or in death to come can ever separate us from that.

Thank you to all who have listened to me over the years, especially my wife, Xavia, and our children, Jennifer and Andrew. No one should have to listen that much! Thank you to three congregations who have called me and paid me for the privilege: The Presbyterian Church in Sudbury, Massachusetts, The Market Street Presbyterian Church in Lima, Ohio, and now The Georgetown Presbyterian Church in Washington DC. Thank you to the many colleagues and church staff members with whom I've been privileged to minister. Thank you to Elam Davies, the then pastor of the Fourth Presbyterian Church in Chicago, who made me a Presbyterian; and to Bryant Kirkland of the Fifth Avenue Presbyterian Church in New York City who made me a preacher. And thanks again, Bill — you made me a pastor.

— Richard Louie Sheffield

Parable 1

Salt And Light

Matthew 5:13-20

Sometimes I think preachers would do best by getting out of Jesus' way. Sometimes, though, getting out of the way isn't easy. Preachers and listeners alike have preconceived notions, personal agendas, and sometimes circumstances beyond control.

I had one of those recently. A circumstance beyond my control. I was sculling. That's an elegant word for rowing on the Potomac in a skinny boat. I'm taking lessons, and I learned that getting out of the way is one of the things I need to learn. I was nervously rowing just the other side of the Key Bridge when a group of college rowers going a lot faster than me began to approach. I wasn't sure what to do as they came directly toward me, so I did the only thing I knew how to do. I stopped, feathered my oars, which is a fancy way of saying I held them straight and flat so I wouldn't tip over and fall in. I stopped and I waited.

Fortunately, they saw what was happening. As they passed just feet from the ends of my oars one of the women rowers called out, "If you can't do anything else, just yell, and let us know you're there."

I'm going to work on learning to get out of the way so I won't have to yell. Sometimes we need to work on getting out of Jesus' way. Before I take the risk of getting *in* his way, I want you to listen to Jesus again. And as I was trying to do with those other boats, see where he's coming from and figure out what it is you need to learn and do.

11

Jesus said:

*You are the salt of the earth; but if salt has lost its taste,
how can its saltiness be restored? It is no longer good
for anything, but is thrown out and trampled under foot.*
— Matthew 5:13

Jesus said:

*You are the light of the world. A city built on a hill can-
not be hid. No one after lighting a lamp puts it under
the bushel basket, but on the lampstand, and it gives
light to all in the house. In the same way, let your light
shine before others, so that they may see your good
works and give glory to your Father in heaven.*
— Matthew 5:14-16

Jesus said:

*Do not think that I have come to abolish the law or the
prophets; I have come not to abolish but to fulfill. For
truly I tell you, until heaven and earth pass away, not
one letter, not one stroke of a letter, will pass from the
law until all is accomplished. Therefore, whoever breaks
one of the least of these commandments, and teaches
others to do the same, will be called least in the kingdom of heaven; but whoever does them and teaches them
will be called great in the kingdom of heaven. For I tell
you, unless your righteousness exceeds that of the
scribes and Pharisees, you will never enter the kingdom of heaven.* — Matthew 5:17-20

Sometimes Jesus taught sitting in a boat, his listeners sitting
on the dock or on the shore. In Luke's gospel it says that one time,

*[Jesus] got into [a boat], the one belonging to Simon,
and asked him to put out a little from shore. Then he sat
down and taught the people from the boat.*
— Luke 5:3 (NIV)

In my case, that would make for much shorter sermons. But in this case, the lesson from Matthew, Jesus was on dry land. What I read is a part of what is sometimes called "The Sermon on the Mount" because Matthew says Jesus was sitting on a hillside.

Sitting there on solid ground he looked around at some folks who were often "at sea" when it came to the living of their lives. I looked up "at sea" for you. It means:

> **at sea** — adj. 1: perplexed by many conflicting situations or statements; [syn: baffled, befuddled, bemused, bewildered, confounded, confused, lost, mixed-up][1]

Jesus said to those on the hillside, whose lives were like that: "You are the salt of the earth," but if you aren't salty, what good are you?

"You are the light of the world," but if your words and deeds don't enlighten anyone as to the truth about life, well that kind of "light" is spelled "l-i-t-e" (as in Bud). The lumens are low. It leaves the truth hidden and the one in need of truth in the dark. What good is that?

The dictionary defines "salt of the earth," to mean: "An individual or group considered as representative of the best or noblest elements of society."[2] Certainly salt was seen as an important element in Matthew's day and time. Salt has various meanings throughout the scriptures, "Including sacrifice, loyalty and covenant fidelity, purification, seasoning, (and) preservative."[3]

If Jesus is saying you are those who put others ahead of self, loyal people who stick to your commitments, people without mixed motives, the spice of life, people who hold onto what is good and true, that's quite a compliment. But Jesus' words, "You are the salt of the earth," aren't so much a compliment as a job description. We're supposed to be those kinds of people, and if we aren't, *who will be?*

One of the commentaries I consulted had a footnote I found helpful in understanding what it means to be "the salt of the earth." It refers to the early Christian writer, Ignatius, and says that, "There may be (here in Jesus' saying) a specific reference to salt's being used as a catalyst for fueling earthen ovens. When such salt lost its catalyzing potency, it was thrown out."[4]

High school chemistry was a long time ago, but I remember that a catalyst is something that makes something happen. Whatever was happening in those first-century earthen ovens, what Jesus was talking about was what happens in life — and about whether you and I are helping make it happen. It's about whether or not we're "catalysts" for the kingdom of heaven.

The dictionary defines a "catalyst" in the human sense as, "A person whose talk, enthusiasm, or energy causes others to be more friendly, enthusiastic, or energetic."[5]

That's the kind of person you and I are called to be — that's why Jesus called his followers "the salt of the earth."

John Newbern said, "People can be divided into three groups: those who make things happen, those who watch things happen, and those who wonder what happened."[6]

"You are the salt of the earth," said Jesus. Make things happen for the kingdom of heaven! Be like Bernard Shaw who wrote,

> *People are always blaming their circumstances for what they are. I do not believe in circumstances. The people who get on in this world are the people who get up and look for the circumstances they want, and if they cannot find them, make them.*[7]

"You are the salt of the earth," said Jesus. You are the catalyst for the kingdom of heaven. So be salty!

"You are [also] the light of the world," said Jesus. That's a rather startling notion, given that in John's gospel, *Jesus* is the "light of the world." John says of Jesus, "The true light, which enlightens everyone, was coming into the world" (John 1:9). You're not Jesus, but you're *like* Jesus. Jesus said so, right there on the side of that mountain.

C. S. Lewis and Luther agreed that the whole purpose of being a Christian is to become a little Christ. Become one who in word and deed embodies the presence of God in this world and enlightens this world with his truth.

When I was a child in Sunday school, we used to sing a song that began, "This little light of mine, I'm gonna let it shine! Hide it under a bushel? No! I'm gonna let it shine!"

That's not just a child's song. It's an African-American spiritual. It is in hymnbooks for grownups to sing, too. Stanza 4 always intrigued me: "Shine all over Chi - ca - go, Yes! I'm gonna let it shine." I wasn't sure why Chicago? The other day I looked it up. I have one of those old hymnbooks. The asterisk by Chicago says "Substitute local name." You might say, "Shine where you are" or "Shine all over Wash - ing - ton?" Too hokey?

Okay, Jesus said it best anyway: "Let your light shine before others, so that they may see your good works and give glory to your Father in heaven" (Matthew 5:16), and not just *for* your good works, but *through* their own. Again, we're called to be a catalyst, not to do everything ourselves, but to see what we do multiplied through the doing of others, who in the light can also see what needs doing.

Sometimes I think we task-oriented types known as Presbyterians, who get things done by doing them, are hesitant to "toot our own horn," or better, "shine our own light" in such a way that we get others to join us. We're not to shine our light on ourselves so folks will applaud us, but rather, shine our light on our works so that others will will see ways in which they, too, can serve.

We've been having trouble at home with my wife's inkjet printer. After a lot of frustration I read the instructions. We had just installed a new ink cartridge and the printer wanted to "align the print head" so the print would be clear. The alignment process is automatic when it works. It wasn't working. The instructions said to start the process and then look inside the printer where the paper comes out while its printing the alignment page. I got down on my hands and knees, pushed the button and waited. The instructions said to look for a blue light shining on the page as it was printing. And then said, "If this light is not present, the unit will not be able to align the cartridges."

The paper started printing. But no blue light was shining. So the work that needed doing couldn't be done.

Jesus suggested, in terms his hearers could understand, pretty much the same thing. The work of the kingdom somehow requires that you and I "shine." That's what Jesus *meant* by "let your light shine." Shine light on opportunities to serve, on the work that needs to be done, and in doing so give glory to God.

In a sense, this is about as close as Jesus comes to the dictum of the writer of the book of James, that "faith without works is ... dead" (James 2:26). Faith that does not work itself out in life is deadly. If nothing else, it's deadly dull. Faith that turns in on itself is self-serving. There's a lot of that around these days. Faith that does not *serve* Christ, one might argue, *is not faith*, or at the least, when that happens, we are not faithful.

Right after Jesus' comments about salt and light, Matthew puts Jesus' words about God's law. There were those in the Jewish community who thought that Jesus' way of doing things was opposed to God's way of doing things. They said he broke God's law. Jesus said he *fulfilled* God's law. Jesus' focus was not on the "letter" of the law, but on the "spirit" of the law. God's intentions, over against human interpretations. The letter of the law would never change, said Jesus, not "one jot or one tittle" (Matthew 5:18 KJV) — but neither, said Jesus, would God's love.

Legalism and love have a hard time coexisting. A lot of Christian history unfortunately proves that. The Pharisees of Jesus' day had trouble with that; with the tension between law and love. The Pharisees, with whom Jesus was so often at odds on this subject, were really Jews with whom Jesus had much in common. The Pharisees were the Jewish party or "denomination" that believed in the resurrection of the dead. Their central belief would become the central truth of Christianity. They were precisely the kind of people the dictionary calls "the salt of the earth." They represented the best and the noblest elements of their society. *We* should be so good — you and I.

But good wasn't "good enough" and still isn't. Whatever our part might be in building the kingdom of heaven, it takes more than just being good. It takes being salt. It takes being light. It takes being like Jesus Christ.

16

But that said, ponder this: Jesus didn't say, "You *need to be* salt. You *ought to be* light. You *have to be* both." He said, "*You are!*"

It dawned on me this week, in the middle of the Potomac. I keep thinking, "I want to be a rower, like those college kids passing me by." Sitting there in the boat, with oars in my hands, left hand over right, oars feathered to keep from flipping the boat — it occurred to me — *you are.*

So reach, and row! Jesus said, "You *are* salt. You *are* light." Be salty and shine! It will give glory to your Father in heaven.

———————

1. http://dictionary.reference.com/search?q=at%20sea.

2. *The Random House Dictionary of the English Language* (New York: Random House, 1966).

3. *The New Interpreter's Bible*, Vol. 8 (Nashville: Abingdon Press, 1995), p. 181.

4. *Ibid.*

5. *The Random House Dictionary of the English Language* (New York: Random House, 1966).

6. Source unknown.

7. Source unknown.

Easter 4

Parable 2

Why Sheep?

John 10:1-10 (Luke 16:19-31)

Why sheep?

For one thing, next week will be Youth Sunday, so I moved things up a week. Next Sunday, which I decided to move up to this Sunday, is called "Sheep Sunday" by preachers, because every year about this time the lessons are like this morning — John's description of Jesus, the good shepherd, and the psalmist's song is "The Lord Is My Shepherd."

But, I wondered out loud to myself this week, why *sheep*? Why not eagles? Why not think of you and me as eagles in God's glorious sky, instead of sheep in God's muddy pasture?

Isaiah writes ...

> *Those who wait for the Lord shall renew their strength,*
> *they shall mount up with wings like eagles, they shall*
> *run and not be weary, they shall walk and not faint.*
> — Isaiah 40:31

That's why I have a plaque on the wall in my office with those words. That's why I love the following hymn. It goes:

> *You who dwell in the shelter of the Lord,*
> *who abide in his shadow for life,*
> *say to the Lord: "My refuge,*
> *my rock in whom I trust!"*

19

And I will raise you up on eagles' wings,
bear you on the breath of dawn,
make you to shine like the sun,
and hold you in the palm of my hand.[1]

Why *not* eagles? Why sheep?

Maybe it's because the prayer of confession got it right — got *us* right: "Almighty and merciful God, we *have* erred and strayed from your ways like lost sheep. We *have* followed too much the devices and desires of our own hearts...."

We seldom soar like eagles; more often we act like sheep. As one old song puts it:

> *We are poor little lambs*
> *who have lost our way ...*
> *Baa! Baa! Baa!*
> *We're little black sheep who've gone astray,*
> *Baa! Baa! Baa!*
> *Gentlemen-rankers out on the spree,*
> *damned from here to eternity,*
> *God ha' mercy on such as we,*
> *Baa! Baa! Baa!*

Some of us are old enough to remember that as the "Whiffenpoof Song," popularized in the '30s and '40s by the singer Rudy Vallee. It was originally part of a poem by Rudyard Kipling. It would make a great prayer of confession, if we could sing it or say it with a straight face. Let's try it. Repeat after me.

> *We're poor little lambs who've lost our way.*
> *We're little black sheep who've gone astray.*
> *God have mercy on such as we!*
> *Baa! Baa! Baa!*

But whatever our words, our confession is still only a refrain to our lives, as Kipling's words are only the refrain to his poem. Kipling's poem reads, in part, like too many lives:

20

We have done with Hope and Honour,
we are lost to Love and Truth,
We are dropping down the ladder rung by rung,
And the measure of our torment
is the measure of our youth.
God help us, for we knew the worst too young!
Our shame is clean repentance
for the crime that brought the sentence,
Our pride it is to know no spur of pride,
And the Curse of Reuben holds us
till an alien turf enfolds us
And we die, and none can tell Them where we died.
We're poor little lambs who've lost our way,
Baa! Baa! Baa![2]

We have erred and strayed — *like lost sheep.* I know that. You
know that. The Bible knows that, and uses that as a metaphor for
the reality of our lives, lives we live together in our families, at our
work, in our community, in this church, every day. And it's our life
lived together that the Frugal Gourmet, Jeff Smith, sees as explaining why the metaphor for you and me is "sheep."

Some of you know Jeff Smith's recipe books. One of them
serves up some wonderful sounding recipes for lamb chops, grilled,
with mint and cinnamon, in grape leaves; and lamb stew with figs
and wine. The Frugal Gourmet says the sheep metaphor in the Bible
finds its meaning in the fact that:

> *Sheep are communal by their very nature. [Pointing out*
> *that] As a matter of fact we do not even have a word for*
> *one sheep. The term is always understood to be plural.*[3]

I'm skeptical of anyone who writes of the love of God for his
"sheep," and how to cook lambchops in the same book. But maybe
the Frugal Gourmet, who happens to be a Methodist minister, as
well as a good cook, is right. The meaning of the metaphor is simply that you and I *together,* like sheep — plural — are a community, a flock of faith in which we are cared for by God as a shepherd cares for his sheep. We're in it together, and together we are
shepherded by Jesus Christ.

21

That's a good corrective to the excessive individualism of our day that leaves many of us feeling so very much alone in the presence of almighty God. We feel more like a sheep at the mercy of a predator than a lamb in God's arms of protection provided in Jesus' story by the sheep being together in the sheepfold — not just in his willingness to run around willy-nilly to find lost ones.

The nineteenth-century Princeton theologian, Benjamin Breckinridge Warfield, whose work was to have great influence on the original "Fundamentalists," apparently considered this to be fundamental: That in Jesus Christ, God was "saving the world and not merely one individual here and there out of the world."[4] In Jesus Christ, God came as a shepherd to his sheep — *plural*.

The children's poem says Mary had a "little lamb." And the classic picture of Jesus, the good shepherd, has him carrying a single lamb on his shoulders. As though he has *a* little lamb, too. But the biblical picture has him surrounded by an uncountable herd of sheep. To paraphrase the children's book by Wanda Gag, there are sheep here, sheep there, sheep and little lambs everywhere. Hundreds of sheep, thousands of sheep, millions and billions and trillions of sheep. All acting like sheep and in need of a shepherd.

So Charles Cousar writes:

> *The language [in John's gospel] is reminiscent of the Twenty-third Psalm. What is eloquently sung there about the Lord's care, guidance, and protection of the flock is here [in John] reaffirmed in terms of Jesus.*[5]

As one writer says,

> *... sure, it's possible to encounter Christ anywhere, but the biblical witness is that that encounter is most likely to happen in a place where people are gathered....*[6]

People gathered, like sheep in a sheepfold, are those most likely to encounter the shepherd. People gathered like sheep in a sheepfold *can be shepherded* — brought together in warmth and the safety of life together.

I did a little research. I read a book called, *Approved Practices in Sheep Production*, that says, that in caring for sheep,

> *... most important is that ... continuous attention [is] required. Sheep are often quite helpless and fall easy prey to predators, especially dogs, coyotes, foxes, bobcats, and eagles. They might even fall prey to such hazards as picket or woven wire fences, or to ditches and gullies in which they might lie and suffocate unless aid came quickly. Parasites and disease are also ever present problems to guard against.*[7]

The book says sheep have a lot of problems. *So do we.* Sheep face a lot of dangers. *So do we.* Sheep are best tended together. Says the Bible, *so are we.* But then what about *me? Me?*

I remarked to some recently that I find it interesting, and telling, that it was about the time we discovered that the sun does not revolve around the earth, that we decided that the universe revolves around the individual. The individual is important, hence the biblical picture of Jesus seeking out that one lost sheep. The image of the sheepfold and you and me as sheep, is not intended to make us feel sheepish, or to make us feel individually *un*important; rather it is intended to reinforce the importance of each and every one of us, *all* of us, to the shepherd who is God in Jesus Christ.

The sheepfold, then, while constraining and confining is not claustrophobic. Rather, by setting limits on how far we can stray, and what can get at us, it frees us to live life as God intends — to live each day to the fullest. This is what Jesus meant when he said,

> *I came that they might have life, and have it abundantly.*
> — John 10:10

> *I came so that everyone would have life, and have it in its fullest.* — John 10:10 (CEV)

Some of the fullest moments of my ministry have been moments filled by folks like you. I had such a moment not too long ago, when someone shared a poem with me that has meant much to them. It's called "Live Each Day To The Fullest," and describes what life lived that way might look like. It goes:

> Live each day to the fullest
> Get the most from each hour, each day, and each age of
>   your life.
> Then you can look forward with confidence and back
>   without regrets.
> Be yourself — but be your best self.
> Dare to be different and to follow your own star.
> And don't be afraid to be happy.
> Enjoy what is beautiful.
> Love with all your heart and soul.
> Believe that those you love, love you.
> Learn to forgive yourself for your faults, for this is the
>   first step in learning to forgive others.
> Listen to those whom the world may consider uninter-
>   esting, for each person has, in himself, something
>   of worth.
> Disregard what the world owes you, and concentrate
>   on what you owe the world.
> Forget what you have done for your friends, and re-
>   member what they have done for you.
> No matter how troublesome the care of life
>   may seem to you at times,
>   this is still a beautiful world —
> and you are at home in it,
>   as a child is at home in his parent's house.
> When you are faced with a decision,
> make that decision as wisely as possible —
>   then forget it.
> The moment of absolute certainty never arrives;
> ... act as if everything depended upon you, and
> pray as if everything depended upon God....[8]

If you live like that, if I live like that, and even when we can't, we can depend upon God, the good shepherd, whom we know in Jesus.

24

I wonder how things might have turned out if the rich man in Jesus' story had lived like that? If he had understood himself to be just one of the sheep in God's fold?

Whatever you make of the rich man's predicament in the parable, his money wasn't worth a dime in death. It won't be to you either. But it will matter to others — it can matter a lot to those you love — family, friends, the faithful flock we call church, your fellow sheep.

The rich man's sin was not being rich. Andrew Carnegie, a Presbyterian, once said that "It is a sin to die rich." You might ponder that some time. But even he never said it was a sin to *be* rich.

I walk a lot back and forth around Georgetown and across the Key Bridge. I walk past a lot of men. It is mostly men, who like Lazarus lie waiting even in one of the richest zip codes in the United States for someone to give them something. I'm urban savvy; not what my children would call "street smart," but smart enough to know that a hand-out isn't always a helping hand. Most of the time I am inured by all the other times I've walked past such men — to the point that like the rich man in the story I hardly see them anymore. Sometimes I look furtively in their direction — mostly to protect myself.

Last week, walking across the bridge, I glanced at a man, barefoot, dirty, half my age, holding a sign. It said the usual: "Have wife and kids. No work. Need help. God blessed you." Have you seen those? I kept going. But I couldn't get the sign out of my mind. I still can't.

And I don't think you heard why — I don't think you heard what I said. You heard what you *thought* I said. You've heard it, seen it, before. What you thought I said was: "Have wife and kids. No work. Need help. God *bless* you."

But that's not what *his* sign said and not what I said. His sign said — listen closely — "Have wife and kids. No work. Need help. God *blessed* you."

I don't know about his wife and children. I don't know why he can't or won't work. I don't know for sure what kind of help would really help. I don't even know if the way he worded his sign was just bad grammar. But I do know he has me dead to rights when he says, "Dick, God *blessed* you!"

I can just hear Lazarus, outside the rich man's gate, day after day watching the rich man go for his aerobic turn around town, saying, "Dives, God *blessed* you!" And Dives, as in the anthem earlier, replying, "Thou art none of mine, brother Lazarus, / Lying begging at my door."[9]

Long before I arrived on the scene, the Georgetown Presbyterian Church committed itself to a better answer than that. The church committed to meeting the needs of those lying at our door. In this neighborhood where the other day I saw something that even around here is unusual — a stretch Rolls Royce — we have joined with other congregations to create and support the Georgetown Ministry Center, a ministry to the homeless in our midst, through which we recognize the man with the sign as "one of ours," as one of God's ... one of God's sheep.

Let's be honest. We'd like to have the man (or the woman) with the Rolls as a member — as one of *our* flock. God chooses to have the man with the sign as one of his too.

You can respond to the man's sign in many ways. One way to respond to the fact that God has blessed you is with your will. God *has* blessed you. God *has* blessed me. I looked it up. The fifth definition of "bless" in the dictionary is: "to confer well-being or prosperity on." God has done that for us. The fourth definition of "bless," however, is: "to honor as holy; [to] glorify."[10] You see, we can bless God too! And one way to do that is with a will. A will that is not just a way of getting what we want in the end; but a way of praying in life and in death the prayer of those who belong to God — *"Thy will be done."*

Someday, somewhere, someone like me will pray. You will be there, but will not hear it. The prayer will go: "Into your hands, O merciful Savior, we commend your servant. Acknowledge, we humbly pray, a sheep of your own fold, a lamb of your own flock, a sinner of your own redeeming." Then they'll go have cookies and punch, and if they haven't already, they'll go read your will.

The hymn, "Take My Life And Let It Be," is usually a "Stewardship Sunday" song, but it's really a hymn about life — life in the sheepfold lived well. Pay close attention to stanza 4.

> *Take my will, and make it thine;*
> *It shall be no longer mine.*
> *Take my heart, it is thine own,*
> *It shall be thy royal throne,*
> *It shall be thy royal throne.*[11]

---

1. "You Who Dwell in the Shelter of the Lord," *With One Voice*, 779.

2. Rudyard Kipling, "Gentlemen-Rankers," *Barrack-Room Ballads* (New York: Signet Classics, 2003).

3. Jeff Smith, *The Frugal Gourmet Keeps the Feast* (New York: William Morrow & Co., 1995), p. 20.

4. Bradley J. Longfield, *The Presbyterian Controversy* (New York, Oxford University Press, USA, 1993), p. 45.

5. Walter Brueggemann, Charles B. Cousar, Beverly R. Gaventa, James D. Newsome, *Texts for Preaching*, Cycle A (Louisville, Kentucky: Westminster John Knox Press, 1995), p. 290.

6. John Wurster, Sermon preached at Market Street Presbyterian Church, Lima, Ohio, 4/21/96.

7. Elwood M. Juergenson, *Approved Practices in Sheep Production* (Vero Media Inc., 1981), p. 6.

8. S. H. Payer, "Live Each Day to The Fullest," source unknown.

9. Andrew Carter, "Dives and Lazarus," *Traditional English Carol.*

10. http://dictionary.reference.com/search?q=bless.

11. "Take My Life, and Let It Be Consecrated," *The Hymnbook*, 310.

Parable 3

Fairy Tale Or God's Word?

Matthew 7:21-29

When we ordain elders and deacons and ministers in the Presbyterian Church we ask a number of questions. Many of you have answered them as you have accepted leadership in this or another congregation.

One of those questions reads:

> *Do you accept the Scriptures of the Old and New Testaments to be, by the Holy Spirit, the unique and authoritative witness to Jesus Christ in the Church universal, and God's Word to you?*[1]

I've formally answered that question five times: when I was ordained a deacon; when I was ordained a Minister of Word and Sacrament; when I was installed as the pastor of the Presbyterian Church in Sudbury, Massachusetts, right out of seminary; when I was installed as the pastor of the Market Street Presbyterian Church in Lima, Ohio, over twenty years ago; and recently when I was installed as pastor here. And I'd like to think I've also answered that question informally, not just in words but in deeds many times over:

> *Do you accept the Scriptures of the Old and New Testaments to be ... God's Word to you?*

Do you believe it? Do you take it seriously? I do! So it was with some hesitancy that I decided to tell you that whenever I read God's word, Jesus' words, in the gospel lesson for today, what comes to mind is the story of "The Three Little Pigs." It is a fairy tale — the fictional account of three pigs who came into some money and had lifestyle choices to make.

One built a house of straw. One built a house of sticks. The other a house of bricks. You know the story. The little pig who built the house of straw and the little pig who built the house of sticks got their houses built fast and then partied. They partied while laughing at the third little pig who engaged in the backbreaking labor of building his house out of bricks. According to Disney, at least, while the third little pig grunted and groaned under the weight of his work, the other two were singing, "Who's afraid of the big bad wolf?" Then the big bad wolf showed up one day. One by one, he stopped in on his potential barbeque dinners, saying, let me in, or "I'll huff and I'll puff and I'll blow your house down!" We all know what happened to the first pig and the second pig. And we *admire* the foresight of the third pig.

I went to the internet, called up Google, and typed in "three little pigs." I got about 5,100,000 responses — all the way from the traditional story, to an economics education site where children in grades K-2 can study the story of the three little pigs to learn about cost benefit analysis, to a site where they offer a barbeque sauce that will help turn your holiday cook-out from "Ho-Hum to Hog Heaven."

You get the idea. It's a story with a moral. It's a story about how hard work is worth it. It's a story about how planning pays off. It's a story about life being more than a lark. It's a story about life that most of us learn the hard way and then try to pass on to our kids to make their lives easier — only to watch them learn the hard way, too.

But still we tell the story. Jesus was first and foremost a master storyteller. And one day Jesus told a story, not about three little pigs, but about two grown men — a wise man and a foolish man. We might want to say a man with common sense and a man with no sense at all.

There was a man who set about building a new house *the easy way*. He built his house on sand where it was easy to dig. And there was another man who built his house the hard way, on hard rock — hard to dig out, hard to handle, hard to haul away.

"Hardly worth the trouble!" the other man might say. But then trouble came. It started to rain. And as the children's song puts it, "The rains came down and the floods came up." The wise man's house stood firm, but the foolish man's house went "splat!"

It's a story with a moral. It's a story about how hard work is worth it. It's a story about how planning pays off. It's a story about life being more than a lark. It's a story about life that most of us learn the hard way and then try to pass on to our children to make their lives easier — only to watch them learn the hard way, too.

I just said that. But that said, Jesus' story is about more than that. Jesus' story is more than a moralistic tale we tell our children in hopes they will do better than we did.

Jesus' story is *God's word*, spoken in a world where "Who's afraid of the big, bad wolf?" is anybody with any sense — anybody with a television or a newspaper or an internet connection.

We've just moved into the manse next door. Don't all of you drop by at once! We now have Comcast Cable TV. We have hundreds of channels to pick from. Someone in the office said, "Yeah, but there's still nothing on, right?" Wrong! What's on every News Channel is word that the wolf is at the door, a truth from which everything else that's on tries to distract us. Jesus' story is God's word spoken to a world where the wolf at the door blows up our children on the pretext of serving God; and the bigger, badder, godless wolf in North Korea plays childish games with adult consequences that could blow us all away.

Jesus' words speak to the world of William Tecumseh Sherman. Sherman knew the world of war. He knew the wolf at the door personally — as have so many others we will remember tomorrow.

On this Memorial Day Weekend as we remember the men and women who over the years have given their lives so that we might live in freedom in this war-weary world, we perhaps can honor their memory best by remembering not just the glory but the reality in which they lived and died.

31

General William Tecumseh Sherman, who served his country during the Civil War, or as we sometimes heard it called south of here, "the recent unpleasantness," said this on June 19, 1879:

> *I am tired and sick of war. Its glory is all moonshine. It is only those who have neither fired a shot nor heard the shrieks and groans of the wounded who cry aloud for blood, more vengeance, more desolation. War is hell!*[2]

Sherman would know!

What you and I know is that sometimes it seems our lives are hell too. The world has gone to hell and so have we. Jesus' story says there is a way you have to live if life is to be worth living in a world like that; in a world like *this*.

The story of the houses built on sand and rock is not a children's story. It's a grown-up story, told to grown-ups and placed where it is in Matthew's gospel to underline what comes before it. The gospel of Matthew is organized around what are called "the five discourses of Jesus." The story gains its meaning in its context.

The story of the wise man and the foolish man and their construction projects concludes the first discourse that covers chapters 5, 6, and 7. This first discourse begins with the Beatitudes and ends with this story which says simply, *are the foundations on which you are building your life secure?* Or will the next big storm take you down?

I looked back through those three chapters preceding Jesus' story to see what a firm foundation for life would look like, according to Jesus. What's he talking about — this difference between building life on rock or sand?

In the discourse, there are personal teachings about anger and adultery and divorce and the havoc they play with our lives. Then there is this: "You have heard that it was said, 'You shall love your neighbor and hate your enemy.' But I say to you, Love your enemies and pray for those who persecute you" (Matthew 5:43-44). Do we?

How about this: "Do not store up for yourselves treasures on earth, where moth and rust consume and where thieves break in and steal; but store up for yourselves treasures in heaven" (Matthew 6:19-20). Do we?

Jesus said to his followers: "Do not worry about your life, what you will eat or what you will drink, or about your body, what you will wear. Is not life more than food, and the body more than clothing?" (Matthew 6:25). How are we doing?

I get emails almost daily from various health-oriented websites like WebMD telling me all the ways stress and worry will do me in. Why would I listen to them if I won't listen to Jesus? Jesus, who said to build a better life:

> *Do not judge, so that you may not be judged. For with the judgment you make you will be judged, and the measure you give will be the measure you get.*
> — Matthew 7:1-2

I think that's the biblical equivalent of "What goes around comes around!"

Eugene Peterson puts those words of Jesus this way:

> *Don't pick on people, jump on their failures, criticize their faults — unless of course you want the same treatment. That critical spirit has a way of boomeranging ... Here is a simple, rule-of-thumb guide for behavior: Ask yourself what you want people to do for you, then grab the initiative and do it for them.*
> — Matthew 7:1-2, 12a (The Message)

How are you doing? Where are you building ... your life? On solid rock or sinking sand?

Peterson translates words of Jesus that those little pigs should've heard:

> *Don't look for shortcuts to God. The market is flooded with surefire, easygoing formulas for a successful life that can be practiced in your spare time. Don't fall for*

that stuff, even though crowds of people do. The way to life — to God! — is vigorous and requires full attention.
— Matthew 7:13-14 (The Message)

Don't build with sticks and straw; don't build on sand; that's the way to disaster. God's way is work, but it's worth it, in the end. Anybody who says it's easy is selling sand dunes.

Eugene Peterson, a Presbyterian minister, has a way with words. I wonder how he would tell the story of the three little pigs. This is how he tells the story of the wise and foolish men:

> *[Jesus said] "These words I speak to you are not incidental additions to our life, homeowner improvements to your standard of living. They are foundational words, words to build a life on. If you work these words into your life, you are like a smart carpenter who built his house on solid rock. Rain poured down, the river flooded, a tornado hit — but nothing moved that house. It was fixed to the rock. But if you just use my words in Bible studies and don't work them into your life, you are like a stupid carpenter who built his house on the sandy beach. When a storm rolled in and the waves came up, it collapsed like a house of cards.*
> — Matthew 7:24-27 (The Message)

That's not a fairy tale. That's *God's word* to you (and me)!

---

1. *The Book of Order, G14:0801g.*

2. Various sources.

34

Parable 4

Listen To Yourself

Matthew 13:1-9, 18-23

Sometimes the best way to start reading your Bible is with the footnotes. Sometimes even in English the Bible seems like it's still written in a foreign language. In a way it is. Not just in Hebrew and Greek with a smattering of Aramaic, but even in English it is still in a "language" 2,000 years or more removed from you and me. The language of the Bible reflects the life of the Bible's people and we don't live there. So we need help if we're going to go there in our mind's eye and hear clearly *what* was being said *when* it was being said.

Most of us are not farmers, and most farmers now don't "sow," that's "s-o-w" the way a farmer in Jesus' day did. So, we need to put ourselves in shoes someone walked in 2,000 years ago if we're going to get anyplace with the parable Jesus told saying, "A sower went out to sow."

This week I went first to the Scottish theologian, William Barclay, and then to the footnote in my study Bible for guidance. Barclay wrote,

> *In Palestine there were two ways of sowing seed. It could be sown by the sower scattering it broadcast as he walked up and down the field. Of course, if the wind was blowing, in that case some of the seed would be caught by the wind and blown into all kinds of places, and sometimes out of the field altogether.*

35

*The second way was a lazy way, but was not un-
commonly used. It was to put a sack of seed on the back
of an ass, to tear or cut a hold in the corner of the sack,
and then to walk the animal up and down the field while
the seed ran out. In such a case some of the seed might
well dribble out while the animal was crossing the path-
way and before it reached the field at all.*[1]

Barclay argues elsewhere that the parables of Jesus are extem-
poraneous stories that catch the listeners in a teachable moment,
that they are not well researched term papers (or sermons!). So
there is a good chance that while Jesus was sitting in that boat, he
could point his hearers to a sower (as Barclay described) sowing
seed on the hillside and say, as it says in the Greek, not "a" generic
sower, but "*the*" sower[2] — *that* sower, the one over there, "went
out to sow." "We know that much," said Jesus. "There he is doing
it. Let's look ahead a bit at some likely results of what he is doing."

And then Jesus goes on with his story. But why a story? Why
not just say it straight out? Just say what he wanted to say? I did, a
while back, in a sermon on this text preached in a very different
context. This is what *I* said: "The parable says some seed fell on
rocky ground. Those are those hard-headed people who just don't
get it. Some fell on shallow soil. They get it, but when things get
tough, they get going. They burn out fast. Some seeds fell among
thorns. They really seem to have it together; then things get scratchy
and they give up altogether. Some seeds fell on good soil. But even
among these, there is a disparity of yield. Some do more than others. Some seem better than others. Some give better than others."

In case you can't guess, I was talking about people in the church.
Matthew was, too, in his gospel. Matthew's audience was also
people in the church. But Jesus' audience was his friends and neighbors, relatives, and a good number of people who didn't like him.
The parable was for all of them. But why a parable? I found the
answer to that in a footnote!

In *The New Oxford Annotated Bible* that I use for study, the
footnote to this parable, which really pertains to all Jesus'
parables, provides some guidance. First it says: "*Parables* are

stories describing situations in everyday life which, as Jesus used them, convey a spiritual meaning."[3]

This is not just a story about farming. And Jesus wasn't really talking about the farmer sowing in the distance, but about the listeners sitting right in front of him. He was getting personal. He was getting in their space and even in their face. That's something preachers sometimes do, sometimes to their peril.

Then the footnote says: "In general the teaching of each parable relates to a single point, and apart from this the details may, or may not, have particular meaning."[4] In other words, don't go making stuff up! Don't get too creative with your interpretation.

Most of the time Jesus told his little stories without explanation — he let them speak for themselves. This one, though, some verses later, has an "explanation." Why this one, and not each of them, is not entirely clear. What is clear is that we need to look for *Jesus'* meaning; make Jesus' point, not use his words to make ours.

Then the footnote says, "Jesus used this method of teaching because:"[5]

(a) it gave vivid, memorable expression to his teachings;

Jesus' hearers were far better than you or me at retaining what they heard. They lived long before the "sound byte" and "Sesame Street." But still, Jesus used stories — preachers called them "illustrations" — to make his point and make it stick. It's easier to take home a good story and retell it the next week, than to absorb three points and a conclusion.

(b) [Jesus told parables because] it led those who heard to reflect on his words and bear responsibility for their decision to accept or oppose his claim;[6]

In the military, the dictum for getting something across, or so I'm told, is:

- Tell them what you're going to tell them.
- Tell them.
- Then tell them what you told them.

That's one tactic. Jesus took another. Tell them just enough to get them *to tell themselves*. Telling stories can do that. And what better way is there to get to your point, than to have your hearer get there before you? You can watch that happen with a story.

I watch faces when I preach. Sometimes I see someone asleep. That's okay. We are a sleep deprived society, and if this is the only place you can doze off go ahead and do it! But sometimes I see someone who is clearly a step ahead of me. Or better yet, someone takes a step I don't, either because I don't have time, or I didn't think to go there.

More than once in many years of preaching, someone has come out and commented on some point I made that I didn't make! The first time that happened I went back and checked the recording of the sermon to be sure. And I was right; I hadn't said that. Whatever I actually did say was translated into what someone needed to hear. It's enough to make you believe in the Holy Spirit. Jesus did. And Jesus trusted that Spirit to speak through his stories the truth about his hearers.

> And "(c) [Jesus told parables because] it probably reduced specific grounds for contention by hostile listeners."[7]

How could anyone get upset hearing an itinerant storyteller sitting in a boat talk about a farmer sowing seed up on the hill and musing about what might happen to the seed? People *did* get upset. They got upset when the light bulb went on, probably on the way home, and they realized that Jesus had been talking not just to them, but about them.

Sometimes on a Sunday morning, people heading out the door will remark on the sermon. It's always nice to hear it was a nice sermon. It's even nice to be gently corrected — it means they're listening! It's especially nice, though, as I did last week, to get a note a week later saying, "Pastor, what you had to say about that, said this to me, and I wanted you to know." It says elsewhere in Mark's gospel that "the common people heard [Jesus] gladly" (Mark 12:37 KJV); "... listen[ed] to him with delight" (Mark 12:37). But

38

what they heard with delight, others heard with disgust or disdain. They heard him, alright! But how could they catch him at it when all he did was tell stories?

One of the best storytellers I know of is Marj Carpenter, former moderator of the Presbyterian Church General Assembly. Marj likes to tell the story of an old woman in North Carolina who turned 100.

> *Reporters come and ask you, when you get to be 100, how you got to be 100. And the woman said, "I don't know. I just woke up and was 100!"*
>
> *You could tell the old lady and the reporter got kind of crossways. One of the things he asked her was "Do you go to church?" She said, "Of course I go to church! I've always gone to church! I'm Presbyterian, and I go to church!" And he said, "Oh, and if you weren't Presbyterian what would you be?" She said, "Well, I'd be ashamed!"*[8]

You can tell that one to your Methodist or your Baptist friends! Don't explain; just smile. Sometimes stories make the point better than sermons, or taking ourselves so seriously that others only see red, instead of truth.

Author Philip Pullman, in his Carnegie Medal acceptance speech, said, " 'Thou shalt not' is soon forgotten, but 'Once upon a time' lasts forever."[9]

Jim Trelease, author of *The Read-Aloud Handbook*, who encourages reading stories out loud to children would understand what Jesus was doing. Trelease has said, "Story is the vehicle we use to make sense of our lives in a world that often defies logic."[10]

If you prefer your sermon quotes to be from theologians, Robert McAfee Brown has said, "Storytelling is the most powerful way to put ideas into the world today."[11]

Jesus thought so. He told a lot of them. And the power of them is their ability to transcend the moment of their telling to tell us something about ourselves.

This is the rare, if not the only parable which Jesus told that gets explained.[12] We read the explanation. There is scholarly debate about who's explaining — Jesus, or *maybe* Matthew. It's a *good* explanation. It's a particularly good explanation, I think, of life in the church, which may explain why Matthew included it. But perhaps the "explanation" is not so much what Jesus *said* as what the church *heard* — how the early church *explained* Jesus' little story.

It's a familiar story, the church's interpretation. I quoted my own take on it earlier. This is John Buchanan's take. (John is the pastor of the Fourth Presbyterian Church in Chicago — the church in which I was baptized, the church in which I became a Presbyterian.) I think John reflects this parable in the preface to his book, *Being Church, Becoming Community.* John writes of our church:

> *Our numbers are down. So are our financial resources. Once-viable neighborhood churches struggle with a devastating combination of deteriorating buildings, declining and aging congregations, and skyrocketing costs of everything from postage to health care for the minister. Our national structures are attacked by zealots of the left and right who, with the currently fashionable style of discourse — short on civility, long on strident melodrama — want us either to revolutionize the oppressive structures of society or to withdraw to a pious cloister foreswearing political/social movement of any kind ... The Presbyterian Church (USA) spends an enormous amount of its energy and resources responding to, attempting to mollify, and arguing with its extremes of left and right, and it continues to watch its financial base slip.*[13]

That's not a happy story! In some ways we are an exception here in Georgetown. Looking at you makes me feel old (and I'm only 59!) — and we do lots more baptisms than funerals. But denominationally, the seeds aren't sprouting, the farm's not thriving, and sometimes it seems the donkey has run off with the seed.

And lest it sound like "our" problem, our story alone, for our Methodist, Lutheran, and Episcopalian brothers and sisters in Christ, the story is the same. Jesus would feel right at home.

Correction. Jesus *is* right at home, with the likes of you and me, who on the best of days can be as hard-headed, shallow, fickle,

40

and only sometimes faithful, as anyone else. Individually and denominationally we have problems. Sometimes we *are* the problem.

But, "So?" says Jesus. "Let anyone with ears listen!" (Matthew 13:9). Listen to what? Listen to the story. And listen, especially in this story, to what Jesus *didn't* say. He didn't condemn anyone. He named names, but he didn't call names. That's what you and I do.

Jesus just looked at the seed falling from the hand of the sower and said, "Life is like that. Sometimes it goes to seed. Sometimes it flourishes." It is like that, isn't it? We forget that Jesus had compassion for that.

It's easy to read this parable, and then the explanation of the parable, and *read into them* our anger and our frustration and our righteous indignation at the *obvious* failures of *others* — in church and out. We all do it. God knows (and he does) in the church we do it to each other. Better that we should hear the parable call all of us to hear again the call of Jesus Christ in our own lives. Jesus calls us to look at our lives to discern where *we* have become hard or shallow or fearful in our faith and in what ways we need to be rerooted in it.

One way to do that will take a little work on your part. It is to simply read the parable the way Jesus told it. Close your eyes. In your mind's eye, go sit in the boat. Look on the shore at your friends and neighbors and relatives and a smattering of people who don't like you. All people like you, with their own problems. Tell them the story. Tell it the way you think Jesus told it.

Careful. Don't tell it the way you think he *should* have told it, especially to *him* or to *her*, but the way you would hope he would tell it to you. What's he telling you to tell them? What *he* told them? That he loved them anyway? You can open your eyes, assuming that you followed directions and closed them!

Go home and read the parable and the explanation. Stand and look at yourself in a mirror as you do. Read them angrily. Then read them compassionately — even sadly. Then do what Jesus said: "Listen" (Matthew 13:3) *to yourself.*

1. William Barclay, *The Daily Study Bible, The Gospel of Matthew,* Vol. 2 (Philadelphia: The Westminster Press, 1975), p. 58.

2. *Ibid*, p. 57.

3. *The New Oxford Annotated Bible* (New York: Oxford University Press, 1991).

4. *Ibid.*

5. *Ibid.*

6. *Ibid.*

7. *Ibid.*

8. Thanks to Marj Carpenter.

9. http://www.aaronshep.com/storytelling/quotes.html.

10. *Ibid.*

11. http://www.brainyquote.com/quotes/quotes/r/robertmcaf177916.html.

12. *The New Interpreter's Bible, Matthew* (Nashville: Abingdon Press, 1995). See note 293 on page 305 for a short discussion of whether this text is from Jesus or from another source.

13. John Buchanan, *Being Church, Becoming Community* (Louisville, Kentucky: Westminster John Knox Press, 1996), p. xi.

Proper 11, Pentecost 9, Ordinary Time 16

Parable 5

Explanations Or Truth?

Matthew 13:24-30, 36-43

So, what's that all about? If that's your question about this lesson from Matthew, you're not alone. Jesus' disciples had the same question. "[Jesus], *explain* to us the parable of the weeds of the field" (Matthew 13:36). "Jesus, what's *that* all about?" According to "the rest of the story" the disciples got what they asked for: an explanation. I struggled with that "explanation" this week.

Should I get up and say, "Good people go to heaven and bad people go to hell — end of discussion!" — and sit down? Is that what it says? Even if it is, is that *all* it says? If so, why a "parable"? Why not just say it? Why all that stuff about wheat and weeds? About whether to weed the garden now or wait for the harvest later?

I wonder. And I'm not the only one. Some scholars wonder whether Jesus explained his parable or Matthew did. Whether what we have is Jesus' *explanation* or the early church's *interpretation*.[1]

Not everybody is comfortable asking that kind of question about scripture. I respect that. If you aren't, don't. But do consider this: The truth in parables comes not in "explanation" but in *understanding*. It comes, not in the kind of understanding that comes from having the facts, but the kind of understanding that comes in knowing the truth — and not just abstract truth, but the truth about you. That's the truth a parable gets at.

That's the truth we most often want to obscure with "facts," the truth we try to "explain" away. As anyone who follows politics knows, facts and explanations don't always add up to "the truth, the whole truth, and nothing but the truth." That's why

43

Jesus taught in parables — to get at the truth. These little stories have a way of catching us unawares and confronting us with truths we might otherwise never see: truths about God, truths about you, and truths about me.

A parable doesn't answer our questions, so much as it questions our answers when it comes to what is *true* in life. You don't "explain" a parable; you might say a parable "explains" you.

One author writes:

> In the preaching of Jesus, parables were not vivid deco-
> rations of a moralistic point but were disturbing sto-
> ries that threatened the hearer's ... world — the world
> of assumptions by which we habitually live, the unno-
> ticed framework of our thinking within which we inter-
> pret other data.
>
> Parables surreptitiously attack this framework of
> our thought world itself. This is why they were so dis-
> turbing then and remain so now, and why we are so
> eager to understand them as illustrations of points we
> are comfortable with already, *rather than letting them
> be the disruptive vehicles of a new vision of how things
> are, a vision that challenges our secure world.*[2]

In John's gospel, on Good Friday, Pilate said to Jesus, "What is truth?" I'm convinced that if Jesus had thought Pilate really wanted to know he would have told Pilate a parable.

A story is told to do for us what William Gladstone did for one young man one day. Tom Gillespie, former president of Princeton Theological Seminary told this story.

> When William Gladstone was Prime Minister of Great
> Britain, he was approached one day by the son of a
> close friend. The young man sought counsel regarding
> his career plans.
>
> "First," he explained to Gladstone, "I plan to com-
> plete my studies at Oxford."
>
> "Splendid," replied the prime minister, "and what
> then?"

"Well sir, I then plan to study the law and become a prominent barrister."

"Excellent," said Gladstone, "and what then?"

"Then I plan to stand for election and become a member of Parliament."

"Wonderful," said Gladstone, "and what then?"

"Then, sir, I hope to rise to prominence in the party and be appointed to a cabinet post."

"A most worthy ambition," replied the senior statesman, "and what then?"

"Oh, Mr. Gladstone," the boy blurted out a bit self-consciously, "I plan one day to become prime minister and serve my queen with the same distinction as you."

"A noble desire, young man," said the older man, "and what then?"

"Well sir, I expect that in time I will be forced to retire from public life."

"You will indeed," replied the aging prime minister, "and what then?"

Puzzled by the question, the young man said hesitantly, "I expect then that one day I will die."

"Yes you will, and what then?"

"I don't know sir. I have not thought any further than that!"

"Young man," said Gladstone, "you are a fool. Go home and think your life through from its end."[3]

Listen to Gladstone. Listen to Jesus. "Think your life through from its end."

Jesus told parables to get you and me to do that. I wonder what life would look like if we did. What we would see? What we would see about ourselves? What we would see about our priorities? What we would see about our hopes and our dreams and our ambitions? What we would see about other people? What we would see if we could fast-forward life to the day of our death, and then turn around and look back and rethink the life we had yet to live?

The young man had the "facts" of his life laid out nicely. He had good explanations and big plans. All good, according to Gladstone. But in the end, ask yourself, "When it's all said and done — what then?" Because "what then" is the truth that will affect what you say and do *until then*.

You're a fool if you don't do that. Go home and think your life through from its end, but not so you can live this life just getting ready for the next one — rather, so you can live this life like there *is* a next one! Jesus' parables assume there is. Some of us may be afraid there is. So we don't live the parable — we live the explanation. We get things backward.

We look at the truth about life now with all its pain and sorrow. We look at our lives and the way we live them with all our faults and failings and project all that on life later, as though that's the only truth there is. And we project our reaction to all that on God, expecting him to react to us the way we react to us and to each other.

At its worst that starts to look like life later *depends* entirely on life now, and if you think life *now* is bad, if you've *been* bad, well just you wait and see. You'll get yours!

You've heard those sermons! That kind of thinking turns this life into an entrance exam for the next. Actually, it's more like a placement exam — deciding which place you will be!

But life now is not just a dress rehearsal for life later. It's a gift of God in the here and now, and Jesus came to help us live a life now worth living later. That's the gospel truth — I believe that. So my rule of thumb for reading scripture is simple: If the good news isn't good — read it again.

> *[Jesus] put before them another parable: "The king-dom of heaven may be compared to someone who sowed good seed in his field; but while everybody was asleep, an enemy came and sowed weeds among the wheat, and then went away. So when the plants came up and bore grain, then the weeds appeared as well. And the slaves of the householder came and said to him, 'Master, did you not sow good seed in your field? Where, then, did these weeds come from?' He answered, 'An enemy has done this.' The slaves said to him, 'Then do you want us to go and gather them?' But he replied, 'No; for in gathering the weeds you would uproot the*

wheat along with them. Let both of them grow together
until the harvest; and at harvest time I will tell the reap-
ers, Collect the weeds first and bind them in bundles to
be burned, but gather the wheat into my barn.' "
— Matthew 13:24-30

Stop right there. What does that say? I think it says two simple things — points to two simple truths. I also think the fact we move to what we are afraid it says (explains?) about "last things" so quickly says more about us than about God.

What it *says* — and these are two observations, not two points, so don't get worried — what it *says* is that the world as we know it *is* the world as it is. That's a fact. But it also says the world as it is is not the world as it will be. That's the truth.

It says we live in a world where good grows beside bad. The proof of that is as near as the front page of a newspaper. And the parable says that it's a fact of life. There's no denying evil. It's real.

The parable agrees with the *current* prime minister of England, Tony Blair. He said, "What we are confronting here is an evil ideology ... It is a battle of ideas, of hearts and of minds, both within Islam and outside it."[4]

There is a hymn that describes our reality as "wheat and tares together sown." That's obvious. But the parable doesn't just say the obvious. The parable offers counsel we would do well to heed: to take care lest in trying to root out evil we uproot good as well. That's a great truth. The world is like that. And we should take care lest we respond to that fact as though we were just like the world.

But there's a greater truth in Jesus' little story. The patience of God promising the kingdom of God in spite of it all. The Master made no threat, just a promise:

[That] the Lord our God shall come,
And shall take his harvest home;
From his field shall in that day
All offenses purge away;
Give his angels charge at last
In the fire the tares to cast,
But the fruitful ears to store
In his garner evermore.[5]

47

So, what's that all about? It's about the promise of life in a world made new, where evil will be no more, in a wondrous world that will need no explanation called the kingdom of God. It's about the truth.

The truth we know in the life, death, and resurrection of the parable teller. The greatest parable of all is now before us. It's on the table. What did Jesus say? "He who has ears, let him hear!" He who can taste and touch and see — let him know.

---

1. *The New Interpreter's Bible, Matthew*, Vol. 7 (Nashville: Abingdon Press, 1995), p. 300. Parables in the life of the lhurch. As the parables were handed on and around in the church's teaching and preaching, they were interpreted and modified to address new situations. These post-Easter additions and modifications can often be easily detected (such as 13:18-23, 36-43), but they are not merely to be stripped away to get back to the original parable. They illuminate the ways Jesus' potent message was heard and interpreted as the early Christians struggled to apply it to their own situations after Easter.

2. *Ibid.*

3. Thomas W. Gillespie, "And What Then?" *The Princeton Seminary Bulletin*, Volume XXI, Number 3, New Series 2000.

4. http://www.comcast.net/news/index.jsp?cat=GENERAL&fn=/2005/07/16/180018.html.

5. "Come, Ye Thankful People, Come," words by Henry Alford, 1984; music by George J. Elvey, 1858.

Parable 6

Storytelling

Matthew 13:31-33, 44-52

Jesus loved to tell stories. Much of his teaching was in the form of stories we call parables. I like *this* story.

A minister died and was waiting in line at the Pearly Gates. Ahead of him was a guy who was dressed in sunglasses, a loud shirt, leather jacket, and jeans. Saint Peter addressed this guy, "Who are you, so that I may know whether or not to admit you to the kingdom of heaven?" The guy replied, "I'm Joe Cohen, taxi driver, of Noo Yawk City." Saint Peter consulted his list. He smiled and said to the taxi driver, "Take this silken robe and golden staff and enter the kingdom of heaven." The taxi driver went into heaven with his silk robe and his golden staff, and it was the minister's turn.

He stood erect and boomed out, "I am Joseph Snow, pastor of Saint Mary's for the last 43 years." Saint Peter consulted his list. He said to the minister, "Take this cotton robe and wooden staff and enter the kingdom of heaven."

"Just a minute," said the minister. "That man was a taxi driver and *he* gets a *silken* robe and *golden* staff. I get cotton and wood? How can that be?"

"Up here, we work by results," said Saint Peter. "While you preached, people slept; while he drove, people prayed."

Please stay awake for the next few minutes!

Every week at worship *people pray*. Sometimes it's because life's like a taxi ride in New York City. Some of you know I used to live in New York City. I worked for Citibank on Wall Street, downtown. We reported to a vice president *up*town on Park Avenue. According to Google maps, that's a distance of 6.3 miles.

Late one Friday, as rush hour was in full swing in Manhattan, we realized we had about half an hour to get important papers from Wall Street to Park Avenue. There was no email; no electronic signatures, and a fax wouldn't do. The papers had to be *hand* delivered.

I was appointed. I ran out to the curb, hailed a cab, jumped in the back seat, waved a $20 bill (real money in those days), and said, "That's your *tip* if you get me to Citibank on Park Avenue by 5:30."

Don't ever do that! The New York taxi driver took off. He drove places that weren't meant for driving and I just held on. Half an hour, and *several* prayers later, I got out of the taxi, somewhat shaken, and handed the driver his fare and his tip. I walked into the Park Avenue office at 5:29 swearing I'd never, ever, do that again!

Sometimes life's like that cab ride. And people pray.

Every week, in every service at Georgetown Presbyterian Church people pray.

People pray prayers for help, prayers for loved ones, prayers for peace, written prayers and personal prayers, printed prayers with words we can say together, and heartfelt prayers with words we would never share with anybody.

We pray. Always we pray, "Our Father who art in heaven, hallowed be thy name. *Thy kingdom come*, thy will be done, on earth as it is in heaven."

We call that "The *Lord's* Prayer." We call it that because the Lord taught his disciples to pray like that. Jesus was praying one day, "And after he had finished, one of his disciples said to him, 'Lord, teach *us* to pray ...' " (Luke 11:1). And he did — teaching them what we call "The *Lord's* Prayer." It might be better to call it "The Disciples' Prayer" because they're the ones who prayed it.

Even better, we might call it "The Kingdom Prayer," because that's what those who pray it pray *for*. It's a prayer for the coming of the kingdom of God. That's really what all our prayers are for. That it might be "On earth as it is in heaven," especially when it isn't.

I've been following with you these past few days the continuing events in London. People are praying. I googled "London," and "Prayer," and came up with all kinds of stories about Muslims praying and Christians praying.

The Reverend Judith Maizel Long, assistant general secretary of *Churches Together in Britain and Ireland*, wrote this prayer:

> *God and Creator of all,*
> *In the compassion of Jesus Christ,*
> *And in the tender mercy of the Holy Spirit,*
>
> *We pray for all who have suffered and died in these*
> *   atrocities;*
> *Bind up the physical and mental injuries*
> *Send your peace upon the bereaved.*
>
> *Bless the emergency services and hospital staff,*
> *The police and all those whose vigilance defends us,*
> *Transport workers and officials who clear up the debris.*
>
> *Protect our Muslim neighbours from revenge attacks.*
> *Help us to build communities of good will.*
>
> *We pray that you will bring the perpetrators to repen-*
> *   tance and justice.*
> *Amen.*[1]

When tragedy happens, prayer happens. Jesus didn't have to tell his disciples *to* pray — just *how*. Prayer happens because life happens.

I read a little story recently about an airline trip where the weather got particularly bad and the plane was bumping badly and even the flight attendants were getting nervous. One of the attendants noticed that one of the passengers had "Rev." before his name. As tension mounted, she walked quietly to his seat and leaned over and whispered "Reverend, people are getting very nervous. Could you do something religious?" He thought about it for a minute, then got up, and as the plane continued to lurch from side to side, he took a couple of trays from the galley, and took up a offering!

Why not? The passengers were no doubt *already* praying.

Jesus told his disciples, when you *do* pray, pray like this: "Our Father in heaven, hallowed be your name, *your kingdom come....*"[2] But what does that mean? What are we praying for? The prayer itself tells us.

A prayer for God's kingdom to come is a prayer for God's will to be done "on earth as in heaven"[3] — for life to be in the seeming absence of God — on earth — as we believe it to be in the presence of God — in heaven.

It's a prayer not just for what *we* want, but for what *God* wants. And when our wants and God's will work as one, we experience God's kingdom. That word "kingdom" is somewhat foreign to our modern ears. What it means on its simplest level is that God's in charge and not subject to recall or election. That doesn't sound very democratic but that's because it isn't.

A hymn which has become a favorite of mine begins, "O Lord, you *are* my God and king."

Several years ago, in its adoption of the statement, "Hope in the Lord Jesus Christ" the General Assembly of our church was responding to many in the church who expressed concern about our national church's commitment to belief in Jesus Christ as "the only Savior and Lord."

This is what the Assembly said:

> *Jesus Christ is the only Savior and Lord, and all people everywhere are called to place their faith, hope, and love in him. No one is saved by virtue of inherent goodness or admirable living, for "by grace you have been saved through faith, and this is not your own doing; it is the gift of God" (Ephesians 2:8). No one is saved apart from God's gracious redemption in Jesus Christ. Yet we do not presume to limit the sovereign freedom of "God our Savior, who desires everyone to be saved and come to the knowledge of the truth" (1 Timothy 2:4). Thus, we neither restrict the grace of God to those who profess explicit faith in Christ nor assume that all people are saved regardless of faith. Grace, love, and communion belong to God, and are not ours to determine.*

52

There are some who would dispense with the "yet," but it is critical to who we are — it is an acknowledgment of *whose* we are. We are God's — we are not God.

And so it is for *God's* kingdom, *God's* will, *God's* rule in our lives that Jesus said to pray and for which we *will* pray in a few minutes. We pray for a kingdom that Jesus described in parables, like those I read from Matthew's gospel.

Jesus said, "The kingdom of heaven is like a mustard seed ..." (Matthew 13:31). I was looking for something this week in an office, and I found a whole jar of mustard seeds. I tried to find a way to give each of you one on your bulletin, but nothing worked. Take my word for it. They're small. There are, by my best guess, at least 10,000 of them in this spice bottle. The label on the bottle says, "Mustard seed comes from a plant that thrives in temperate regions. Grown in Canada, it has a hot, pungent flavor. It is referred to as a symbol of faith in the New Testament."

So it is, and one commentator writes:

> *The* parable *of the mustard seed (Matthew 13:31-33) in some ways images the primary theme of the entire chapter. It offers a word of encouragement to those who puzzle about their investment in Christian mission. The reign of God may seem like sheer weakness, no more than an insignificant mustard seed. But take heart. The tiny mustard seed ultimately produces a huge shrub, and God's reign is like that. Don't be deceived by its modest beginnings. Its final consummation will be great.*[4]

The parable is not a promise of greatness. It is not a promise that all things will turn out as I want, but rather, it is a promise that things will turn out as God wants — and that will be great for us all — *that* will be the kingdom of God. A kingdom, says the parable of the treasure in the field and the parable of the pearl of great price, that is worth giving up everything else to attain.

Charles Cousar writes that in both of these parables,

> "... the object found becomes the overriding concern, the concern that crowds out all other concerns. Neither protagonist considers the possibility of passing up the chance to purchase the field or the pearl. The discovery takes precedence over prudence or caution. Living under the reign of God entails discoveries like these, which reshape priorities and result in single-minded devotion."[5]

And just in case you think that can't be until we're all perfect, or at least all on the same page, Matthew appends one more parable:

> The kingdom of heaven is like a net that was thrown into the sea and caught fish of every kind; when it was full, they drew it ashore, sat down, and put the good into baskets but threw out the bad. So it will be at the end of the age.   — Matthew 13:47-49a

When our focus is more on the last part of that parable and doing our own sorting out as to who's in and who's out in the kingdom of God, we miss the point of the first part — which is that God's kingdom comes no matter what and no matter who. If there *is* to be sorting it is for the end of the age and the angels will do it — *not us.*

It is for us to do the work of God's kingdom on earth — plant the seed, till the field, pay the price, and become a living parable of how it will be someday in the kingdom of heaven. It's important that we plant the seed, and leave the "sorting" to God — because too often when we sort we mess up.

I have two parables to make the point. I am told they are true. They are two stories about two Roman Catholic altar boys named Josef and Peter John.

Josef Brose lived in Yugoslavia. At age twelve, he was an altar boy and proud of it. The sanctuary was packed one Sunday morning. Josef took the crystal cruet filled with communion wine and marched proudly up the altar steps. As he got to the top step he tripped, dropped the crystal cruet, and watched as it smashed into 1,000 pieces. He knelt before the priest and said, "Father, forgive me, I have sinned."

The priest looked at Josef and said, "Get out! Get out of this church and don't ever come back again!"

Remember, *this story is true.*

Josef got out, and he never darkened the door of a church again for the rest of his life. Josef Brose grew up to become someone most of you will remember — Josef Brose became Marshall Tito, and under his rule in Yugoslavia the church was oppressed and hundreds of thousands, even millions of people were slaughtered.

Meanwhile, Peter John, also twelve years old, was growing up in Peoria, Illinois. His Roman Catholic church was packed one Sunday morning, *too.* The bishop was there. Peter John was the altar boy and proud of it. Peter John took the crystal cruet filled with communion wine and marched proudly up the altar steps. As he got to the top step he tripped, dropped the crystal cruet, and watched as it smashed into 1,000 pieces.

The bishop looked at Peter John, and then said to the congregation: "Friends, our altar boy, Peter John, has given us a wonderful example of God's redemption and grace. Is there any one of us who hasn't had a shattering experience? Peter John, thank you for giving us an illustration of redemption and the gospel. For when our lives are broken apart in a million pieces, there is a God who can bring resurrection out of crucifixion."

"Peter John, the truth of the matter is that God is going to put your broken pieces back together and make you a stronger altar boy, a stronger Catholic, a stronger Christian. Let me confess *my* sin, Peter John. When I was an altar boy, I, too, dropped a crystal cruet — just like you. I dropped a cruet; you dropped a cruet. Maybe you'll be a bishop, just like me." With that he gave a big wink, and went on with the service.

Peter John grew up and went on to become someone many of you will remember — Bishop Peter John Fulton Sheen. Bishop Sheen was the first Catholic television evangelist and was seen by millions of people on Tuesday evenings in the 1950s. His homilies brought hope to a world of hurt and hatefulness, where peoples' lives are shattered and broken every day.

It's all in the story you tell and how you tell it. Jesus told stories, saying "Let anyone with ears to hear listen!" Listen to the parables you are telling with your life. Are you telling kingdom stories?

1. http://www.ekklesia.co.uk/content/news_syndication/article_05077mcb.shtml.

2. "The Lord's Prayer," Ecumenical.

3. *Ibid.*

4. Walter Brueggemann, Charles B. Cousar, Beverly R. Gaventa, James D. Newsome, *Texts for Preaching*, Cycle A (Louisville, Kentucky: Westminster John Knox Press, 1995), p. 423.

5. *Ibid*, p. 424.

Proper 19, Pentecost 17, Ordinary Time 24

Parable 7

How Many Times?

Matthew 18:21-35

I received a piece of mail not too long ago that brought a rather disconcerting message. The sales piece said: "God May Forgive, But The IRS Won't." It went on to offer, for $3.50, a little booklet titled "17 Most Common Tax Mistakes Ministers Make, What They Are, And How To Avoid Them." I ordered a copy. I just wish there was a booklet to help all of us avoid the one most common mistake *all* of us make all of the time. That mistake is to rewrite the title of that little booklet with our lives to read: "God May Forgive, But *I* Won't."

Or maybe, "*I Can't.*" God may forgive so-and-so for such-and-such, but *me*? Forget it. Do you know how he made me feel? Do you have any idea what she did to me? Do you know what that cost me? Do you know where that leaves me?

The only honest answer I've got is, "No, I don't." I don't know. Only you know that. But I *do* know what it *will* cost you and where it *will* leave you, if you will not or you cannot forgive — you cannot quit counting the cost and leave the accounting to God. You must find freedom for yourself in forgiving others.

The lack of forgiveness by the IRS is a matter of legend. The lack of forgiveness between "me and thee" is a matter of life — my life and yours. Whether we choose to live life letting go of those things that destroy life; or we hold them close and die every day.

Jesus' teaching on forgiveness is actually rather *unforgiving*, in the sense that it leaves us with little, with really *no* choice. Forgive and live, says Jesus. As Lew Smedes writes:

57

Forgiveness is God's invention for coming to terms with a world in which, despite their best intentions, people are unfair to each other and hurt each other deeply. He began by forgiving us. And he invites us all to forgive each other.[1]

Since you've just had someone or something you're not about to forgive come to mind — and if you didn't, you're asleep — we need to ask the obvious question. Matthew says Peter asked it for us:

> *Peter came up to the Lord and asked, "How many times should I forgive someone who does something wrong to me? Is seven times enough?"*
>   — Matthew 18:21 (CEV)

"There's a limit, Lord! So-and-so, or such-and-such, has gone too far. Forgive? Forget it! Enough is enough." I love Peter! God knows, he's just like you and me. He is good-hearted, trying hard, but within limits. I sense in the story we read that Peter had just reached his limit with someone or something. That his was not just a generic or a philosophical question about the abstract nature of forgiveness. Someone pushed his buttons and Peter was pushing back. Now Peter was feeling Jesus out about the need to forgive someone one .... more ... time. And it's someone they both knew.

The Contemporary English Version of Matthew 18:21 says, "How many times should I forgive *someone*...?" The New Revised Standard version says, "someone" is, "... *another member of the church*...." The Greek text says, it isn't just "anyone," it's "... *my brother*...." Peter had a brother. His name was Andrew. Personalize it. "Peter came up to the Lord and asked, 'How many times should I forgive *Andrew*, anyway? Seven times seems more than fair to me!' "

I suspect it seems more than fair to you and me, too. Enough is enough, we say. And seven times is more than enough. But it wasn't enough for Jesus. And his answer to Peter says it isn't enough for you and me, either. Jesus' answer to Peter's question was, "Not just seven times, but *seventy-seven* times" (Matthew 18:22 CEV).

58

And if that isn't bad enough, you can also translate Jesus' words, "not just seven times, but *seven times seventy times*," which, on my calculator comes up to *490 times!* That's a lot. But as Wordsworth puts it in his Ecclesiastical Sonnets:

> *High heaven rejects the lore*
> *of nicely calculated less or more.*[2]

Wordsworth was talking about money and our need to give more. Jesus was talking about forgiveness and our need to forgive more. Incalculably more.

Any debate about "how much more," misses the meaning entirely, as the parable that follows makes clear. The parable is about a man who was a slave. He was owned by the king. And worse, he owed the king — big time. How big? Ten thousand talents! Well, how big is that? I got out my calculator. One "talent" is the biblical equivalent of fifteen years of wages for a common laborer. Let's pay the laborer a "living wage." Mayor Anthony Williams and others say that in the District of Columbia that is $11.80 per hour. Let the work week be forty hours. Ten thousand talents is $24,544 per year for 150,000 years! I had to multiply it out by hand. My calculator went into overload! You can check me. (And I'm sure someone will!) The slave owed his master $3,681,600,000! You've got to give him credit. He said, "Give me time, and I'll pay you 'every cent I owe' " (Matthew 18:26 CEV).

That's over 300 billion cents! I tried to imagine hauling that over to my bank and dumping it into one of those change-counting machines. The amount is absurd. And so is the king's response. *He forgave the debt.* Instead of selling the man, his wife, his children, and everything he had, just to make a down payment on a debt that could never be paid, the king forgave every penny. That's a lot of pennies. A lot of debt. A lot of forgiveness.

According to Jesus, that's the way God forgives you and me. Jesus responded to Peter's counting the petty cash of life, with the amazing truth that we can count on God's forgiveness again and again and again and again and yet again. God's love is without limit. But we limit our experience of it when we limit our love of one another — like the slave in Jesus' story.

Without so much as a thank you, he headed out the door and bumped into another slave who owed him 100 denarii. A denarii was one day's wage. In our example, $94.40. The debt was about $10,000. Not insignificant, but a drop in the piggy bank by comparison to the debt just forgiven. The second slave begged for time in almost the same words spoken by the first slave to the king: "Have patience with me, and I will pay you." But the *forgiven* slave was unforgiving. He sent the second slave to prison "until he could pay what he owed" (Matthew 18:30 CEV). The servant who had been forgiven the impossible, did not find it possible to forgive.

By now, Peter must have been squirming. The message was clear. "Peter, considering how much God has forgiven you, how is it that you can be so *un*forgiving of your brother?" Jesus was not saying that the debt Peter felt he was owed, or the slight he felt he had endured, or the pain he had suffered, was insignificant. It wasn't. And it wasn't just, "Oh, c'mon, Peter — live and let live." It's "Come on, Peter. Forgive. One more time do what God does all the time." Jesus' answer to Peter's question is essentially, "Peter, you can stop forgiving when God does."

What that would look like, for God to quit forgiving, is well described by the end of the parable. When word got back to the king that the forgiven servant was so *un*forgiving he revoked his forgiveness. And the unforgiving servant found himself right back where he started. He was still hopelessly indebted to his master.

It's as though the prayer Jesus taught us to pray had been answered:

- "Forgive us our debts *as we forgive our debtors.*"
- "Forgive us our trespasses *as we forgive those who trespass against us.*"
- "Forgive us our sins *as we forgive those who sin against us.*"
- "Be just as forgiving of us *as we are of others, O God!*"

Someone has said you should be careful what you pray for because you may get it! Do you really want God to be *just* as forgiving of you as you are of others? God knows, I don't. Because I know myself too well. I think we all do.

So the apparent ending of Jesus' parable is hard to swallow. Because the slave was unforgiving, it says, the king took back his forgiveness. Would God do that? To you? To me? No!

That's what I believe about the love of God in Jesus Christ: that God would never not forgive.

Scholars and commentators handle the seeming suggestion that God would withdraw forgiveness from the unforgiving by saying that suggestion is really Matthew's suggestion, not that of Jesus. They say that Matthew elaborated on Jesus' story that *really* ended with the king's question, "Should you not have had mercy on your fellow slave, as I had mercy on you?" (Matthew 18:33). That's really Jesus' question to Peter. "Should you not forgive your brother, as God has forgiven you?"

"Has God forgiven you only seven, or even seven times seventy times, Peter? Or has God forgiven you more times than you can count? And certainly more times than you want to remember? Why should you do any less for your brother?"

I agree with Oswald Chambers, who once wrote:

> God never threatens;
> the devil never warns.[3]

It isn't "Forgive or else," but rather, "How else is there to live except to forgive each other?"

Bob Patterson writes about

> ... Jesus' insistence on forgiveness and reconciliation. Forgiveness is not a law, but a disposition of the heart which we learn from Christ Himself. In his novel, Love Is Eternal, Irving Stone has Mary Todd, the grieving widow of the just-slain Abraham Lincoln, say that she cannot forgive the assassin. Her son, Tad, responds, "If Pa had lived, he would have forgiven the man who shot him. Pa forgave everybody."[4]

Thank God he did. Thank God, God does, in Jesus Christ.

N. T. Wright, the Bishop of Durham in England, has written a book titled, *Simply Christian*. In the religious environment in which we live, where everyone is a liberal or a conservative, or a progressive, or orthodox, or a member of the covenant network, or the lay committee — you name it — it's refreshing, if nothing else, to hear someone call himself simply "Christian." And then go on to articulate in a personal, pastoral, sometimes pointed way what it means to *be* a Christian. Some are saying that the bishop's new book, *Simply Christian*, is simply the best of its kind since C. S. Lewis wrote *Mere Christianity*.

Early on in his book, Bishop Wright acknowledges that being Christian does not always translate easily into being Christlike. That's something Paul had trouble with, too. The bishop writes:

> *There have always been people who have done terrible things in the name of Jesus ... There's no point hiding from the truth, however uncomfortable it may be. It's no part of Christian belief to say that the followers of Jesus have always got everything right. Jesus himself taught his followers [like Peter] a prayer which includes a clause asking God for forgiveness.* He must have thought we would go on needing it.[5]

How many times? As many times as you need!

---

1. Lewis B. Smedes, *Forgive and Forget, Healing the Hurts We Don't Deserve* (San Francisco, California: Harper, 1996), p. xii.

2. William Wordsworth, "Sonnet XLII," *The Ecclesiastical Sonnet of William Wordsworth* (New Haven, Connecticut: Yale University Press, 1922).

3. Source Unknown.

4. Floyd W. Thatcher, Bob E. Patterson, and Elizabeth Rockwood (The Guideposts' Home Bible Study Program) *Discovering Matthew* (Carmel New York; Guideposts Associates, Inc., 1985), p. 111.

5. N. T. Wright, Simply Christian (San Francisco, California: HarperSanFrancisco, 2006), p. 12.

Parable 8

More Than Fair!

Matthew 20:1-16

I ran across a website a while back that said something that we all know, intuitively: "A roll of the dice is not fair." Literally!

According to the website, if you roll a die (that's the singular of dice) 10,000 times, the side with one dot will come up 1,654 times, and the side with six dots will come up 1,679 times. That's not a great difference, but it's enough of a difference to make the casino business immensely profitable. If you play long enough, the casino will win — always. The odds are against you. It isn't fair.

Neither is life. If Hurricane Katrina didn't convince you of that, I have it on no less an authority than Jesus himself. In that sermon he preached "on the mount," Jesus said that "[God] makes his sun rise on the evil and on the good, and sends rain on the righteous and on the unrighteous" (Matthew 5:45). Doesn't sound fair to me. But much of life is like that. Good things happen to bad people. Bad things happen to good people. It's not fair.

In the Old Testament, Job says that in the end of life,

One dies in full prosperity, being wholly at ease and secure ... Another dies in bitterness of soul, never having tasted of good. They lie down alike in the dust and the worms cover them.　　　　　— Job 21:23-26

Is that fair?

The writer of Ecclesiastes said,

In my vain life I have seen everything; there are righteous people who perish in their righteousness, and there are wicked people who prolong their life in their evildoing. — Ecclesiastes 7:15

The Bible is very aware. Life is not fair. And neither, it seems, is God.

I have that on Jesus' authority, too — in that parable I read about the day laborers and the apparent disparity in their pay. Jesus began, "The kingdom of heaven is like ..." (Matthew 20:1). That's a signal that the story to come is not just about heaven, but also about earth.

Jesus taught us to pray, "Thy kingdom come, thy will be done, *on earth as it is in heaven.*" This parable is a story about what the world would be like if that happened. And frankly, it isn't fair. What happened that day would fit no definition of fairness that I can think of.

A landowner hired a group of laborers to work a twelve-hour day at a usual rate of pay. That much was fair. Everybody knew up front what was expected and what they would get out of it. But then the unexpected happened. The first group of laborers had been hired about 6 a.m. About 9 a.m., when that first group had already put in three hours of work, the landowner hired another group. About noon, he hired more workers. About 3 p.m., he hired more. And at 5 p.m., even more. The landowner said to all these later workers in turn, "You also go into the vineyard, and I will pay you whatever is right" (Matthew 20:4). In effect, promising these later hires only that he would be fair.

And if at the end of the day he *had* been fair, he would not have been faulted. Those hired at five would have been happy to get one hour's pay. Those hired at noon, a half-day's pay, and so on. That's all he had to do to be "fair," but he wasn't.

When the group that had worked only an hour was paid first, he was *more* than fair. A *lot* more. They got a whole day's pay! Twelve times more than they had earned! So, too, those who had worked three hours and six hours and nine hours. A full day's pay for them, too. By the time he got to those who had worked all day, who had "borne the burden of the day and the scorching heat" (Matthew 20:12), who had worked twelve full hours, they were expecting a bonus. "They thought they would receive more" (Matthew 20:10). After all, fair's fair! Right? Wrong — apparently.

They all got the same. One day's pay for one day. Twelve hours earlier, those who worked the whole day had considered "the usual daily wage" (Matthew 20:2) to be fair — and were no doubt glad to get it. But now, at the end of the day? "Not fair!" they said. And that is Jesus' point. The kingdom of heaven is not about being fair. It's about being far more than fair — *like God.*

The question we need to ask ourselves is why does this parable rub us the wrong way? Let me suggest it is because we most readily identify in the story with those folks who started work at 6 a.m. We resonate readily with a television ad for a brokerage firm that says, "We make money the old-fashioned way. We earn it!" Presbyterians are not among the richest group of Christians on earth for no reason. The Protestant work ethic pays off.

Presbyterian minister, Ed White, of the Alban Institute has said of you and me that "Presbyterians are self-made people. And as self-made people we have a lot to be proud of but little to be thankful for."

Why is that? Read the story!

Who do you think, in Jesus' story, was most thankful? Who grumbled? Who do you identify with in the story? Interestingly, the grumbling was not about getting more for working more. It was about others getting the same for working less.

"When the first came, they thought they would receive more; but each of them also received the usual daily wage. And when they received it, they grumbled ... saying, 'These last worked only one hour, and you have made them equal to us ...' " (Matthew 20:11-12). The perceived unfairness was not with what *they* got, but with what the others got — more than they "earned." Those who had earned their full day's pay resented that.

But the landowner replied, "What's your problem? You got what you earned! And I did what I wanted with my money. What's it to you?" What it was to them, what it feels like to us, is unfairness. Which it *was*, and it is, *thank* God.

The story is saying that the grace of God is not something any of us can earn. We cannot work our way to the kingdom of heaven. A kingdom where, Jesus said, "The last will be first, and the first will be last" (Matthew 20:16). That, too, sounds "unfair," but it's really *more than fair.*

Play with those words today. The first will be last. The last will be first.

But if the first are last, and the last are first, then the first and the last are both "first." If the parable is an explanation of how that works, then it isn't that the "first" lose, but that the "last" win. Instead of win-lose, which is the way of our world, the kingdom of heaven is win-win. And that's more than just fair.

No? Let me tell you another story.

> There is an old rabbinic parable about a farmer who had two sons. As soon as they were old enough to walk, he took them to the fields and he taught them everything that he knew about growing crops and raising animals. When he got too old to work, the two boys took over the chores of the farm and when the father died, they had found their working together so meaningful that they decided to keep their partnership. Each brother contributed what he could and during every harvest season, they would divide equally what they had together produced. Across the years, the elder brother never married, but stayed an old bachelor. The younger brother did marry and had eight wonderful children.
>
> Some years later, when they were having a wonderful harvest, the old bachelor brother thought to himself one night, "My brother has ten mouths to feed. I only have one. He really needs more of this harvest than I do, but I know he is much too fair to renegotiate. I know what I'll do. In the dead of the night, when he is asleep, I'll take some of what I have put in my barn and I'll slip it over into his barn to help him feed his children."
>
> At the very time the older brother was thinking that, the younger brother was thinking to himself, "God has

66

given me these wonderful children. My brother hasn't been so fortunate. He really needs more of this harvest for his old age than I do, but I know him. He's much too fair. He'll never renegotiate. I know what I'll do. In the dead of the night, when he's asleep, I'll take some of what I've put in my barn and slip it over into his barn for his retirement."

And so one night when the moon was full, as you have already anticipated, those two brothers came face to face, each on a mission of generosity. The old rabbi said that [though] there wasn't a cloud in the sky, a gentle rain began to fall. You know what it was? God weeping for joy because two of his children had gotten the point. Two of his children had come to realize that generosity is the deepest characteristic of the holy and because we are made in God's image, our being generous [our being more than fair] is the secret to our joy as well.[1]

The rabbi had it right. The kingdom of heaven is not fair — it is more than fair — and not just with "them," but with you, and with me.

Albert Einstein once said, "God doesn't play dice with the universe." He doesn't. In the end, it isn't just the luck of the draw or the toss of the dice or the turn of the wheel. In this life, as in every casino, all that is stacked against you. In the end, God is for you in Jesus Christ.

Xavia and I had the privilege of attending the National Day of Prayer and Remembrance Service at the National Cathedral after Hurricane Katrina struck. Readers read. Choirs sang. Bishops and a rabbi and an imam pronounced. T. D. Jakes preached. President Bush spoke. And all of us sang hymns.

The president said, in part, "Americans of every race and religion were touched by this storm; yet some of the greatest hardships fell upon citizens already facing lives of struggle — the elderly, the vulnerable, and the poor. And this poverty has roots in generations of segregation and discrimination that closed many doors of opportunity. As we clear away the debris of a hurricane, let us also clear away the legacy of inequality. Let us deliver a new hope to communities that were suffering before the storm. As we rebuild homes and businesses, we will renew our promise as a land of equality and decency. And one day, Americans will look back at the response to Hurricane Katrina and say that our country grew not only in prosperity, but in character and justice."

I hope and pray it will be as the president has said, because if it is, the American people will be said in our time to have been *more than just fair.*

---

1. http://www.30goodminutes.org/scec/sermon/claypool_4317.htm.

Parable 9

Think!

Matthew 21:23-32

So, what do *you* think?

When Jesus told the parable about the father with two sons to its original audience, they were already squirming after his earlier question to them about John the Baptist. He didn't say to them, "Here's an easy answer." He said, "Here's a hard question!" A hard question in the form of a simple story — a parable. "What do *you* think?"

So, what *do* you think? I don't mean them. I mean *you*.

Parables aren't little Bible stories that provide pious answers to life's problems. They're think-pieces. They're meant to make you think. Every time Jesus told a parable, it was as though he nailed on the wall in front of his hearers one of those signs that used to hang on the walls at IBM. THINK!

You can buy those original signs on Ebay — for $25 and up. According to IBM's internet archives:

> *The "THINK" motto was developed by Thomas J. Watson Sr. three years before he joined the forerunner of today's IBM in 1914. By the early 1930s, THINK began to take precedence over other slogans in IBM, and it appeared on signs ... in IBM plants and offices, and in company publications, calendars, and photographs all over the world.*[1]

(I assume the sign was the origin of IBM's "Think Pad" line of computers.) But before Tom Watson said it with one word, Jesus said it with parables. THINK! And not just about what his stories must have meant to those to whom Jesus told them. Think also about what his stories still mean to those of us who hear them now.

The Bible is great literature. Literary analysis and criticism is helpful. What Jesus was saying to his immediate listeners is always important for us to understand, so we don't misunderstand. But the Bible is also God's word to you and to me. It is important to understand what God is saying to *us*.

We underline that when we install elders, deacons, and pastors to office in the Presbyterian church. We ask those who would lead to affirm what they believe. We do that by asking questions. Among the questions is this one, "Do you accept the scriptures of the Old and New Testaments to be, by the Holy Spirit, the unique and authoritative witness to Jesus in the church universal, and God's word to you?"[2] Not, "God's word to those that heard it spoken," but, "God's word to you to whom God is speaking."

That doesn't mean, "Do you hold to a particular view of biblical inerrancy, or interpretation, or what somebody says is 'fundamental' to the faith?" as some would wish it. It does mean, "Do you believe that, through holy scripture, *God speaks to you?*" That what God has to say is not *embalmed* in a book, but is very much alive in the life of his people, in your life, and in mine?

If the answer is, "Yes," then the question is this, "When God speaks to you, what do you think?" That was Jesus' question to "the chief priests and elders of the people [who] came to him as he was teaching" (Matthew 21:23), to ask him a question. He answered their question with his own question that was intended to make them think. Really, to find within themselves the truth they already knew.

Be careful, though. He didn't say, "Find your own truth." That's something for another sermon another day. It wasn't what would you *like* to think. He said, "What *do* you think?" What do you already know about yourself that you would rather *not* think about right now?

70

Do you ever wonder what got Jesus killed? He had a propensity for asking the right question at the wrong time — for making people think — and then challenging their thinking in a way that made people mad. He made them think the truth about themselves. He often did that, as he did this time, with a parable. A little story told to make you think. Not to be overanalyzed, but to be understood.

Some of the Jewish religious and political establishment of that day were opposed to Jesus and his teaching — you might say, "to his way of thinking." On this particular occasion, instead of challenging his teaching, though, they challenged his authority to teach. It was a political ploy, pure and simple. Discredit his credentials, discredit his teaching, discredit him.

From time to time, in the news we hear of someone who has lost a prominent position, not because they were doing a bad job, but because it was discovered they had exaggerated or lied on their resumes. They really didn't go to that school, or earn that degree and the authority it confers. That day they were checking out Jesus' resume — Jesus' credentials — Jesus' authority — in hopes he wouldn't check out. Then they could check him off their list of problems to be solved. "Show us your credentials, Jesus! Who authorized you to teach here?"

Jesus saw it coming. He knew where they were going. So he put the ball back in their court. Jesus played hardball, too. "I'll tell you what," he said, "you answer my question, *then* I'll answer yours." Apparently they bit. Jesus asked his question. He really just asked them their own question, but about his cousin, John the Baptist. Jesus asked, "By whose authority did John baptize? Did the baptism of John come from heaven, or was it of human origin?" (Matthew 21:25). Were John's words God's words — or just John's? Was God John's authority — or not? What were John (the Baptist's) credentials? What do you think?

Well, one thing's for sure. They didn't think as well on their feet as Jesus. They could have walked away from that loaded question, but instead, they stood there worrying about how to answer. How they answered would affect *their* authority in their religious and political community.

Matthew lets us in on their quandary. They argued among themselves about what to say. "If we say [the authority of John the Baptist was] 'from heaven,' he will say to us, 'Why then did you not believe him?' " (Matthew 21:25). And we don't want to answer that question!

On the other hand, "If we say [John's authority was] 'of human origin,' we are afraid of the crowd; for all regard John as a prophet" (Matthew 21:26), as one who speaks with authority from God.

It was politics as usual. We know what the crowd thinks. We know what the polls say. We know what we think. But we don't want to say what we think. There was a whole lot of thinking going on. But in the end politics, not thoughtfulness, prevailed. "We don't have an answer for you, Jesus." "Well," said Jesus, "then I don't have an answer for you!"

But, "What do you think?" (Matthew 21:28). "Tell me what you think of this story" (Matthew 21:28 The Message). It's just a story.

"A man had two sons. He went up to the first and said, 'Son, go out for the day and work in the vineyard.' The son answered, 'I don't want to.' Later on he thought better of it and went. The father gave the same command to the second son. He answered, 'Sure, glad to.' But he never went. Which of the two sons did what the father asked? They said, 'the first' " (Matthew 21:28-31 The Message).

What else *could* they say? What would you say? What's more important? What you *say*, or what you *do*? What do you think? I suspect that by this time they'd gotten the message and knew they'd been had. But just in case they hadn't, Jesus explained. He compared them in their religiosity, and in their response to John's call to repentance, and in their response to himself and his teachings, to the son who said he would do as the father asked, but then didn't do it. And then he compared "crooks" and "prostitutes" who, the scriptures say, heard both John and Jesus gladly, to the son who said he wouldn't do as his father asked, but then did.

Jesus was saying that his hearers *believed* the right things, and said the right things, but they didn't *do* the right things. John's call to repentance that Jesus said was heard by crooks and prostitutes,

72

but not by the chief priests and elders, as well as Jesus' own teachings, was a word from God to *do* something — not just to *hear* something. Not even just *believe* something, or *say* something, but *do* something about the way they lived their lives.

That's what John and Jesus both meant by "repent!" Go and *do* what the Father has said. And no matter how religious they were, no matter how political they were, said Jesus, they needed to do more than hear the Father's words; they needed to do something in response — and if the words of the Bible are God's word to you and me, so do we!

As we ordain officers in the Presbyterian church, we say a lot of words. I went back and read all the words of "The Constitutional Questions to Officers" again this week in light of the parable. They're words about what elders and deacons and pastors (our "chief priests and elders of the people"), are called *to do*: "Trust, acknowledge, believe, accept, receive, and adopt, be instructed and led, lead, fulfill, be continually guided, be governed, abide, be a friend, follow, love, work, promise, serve, be faithful, watch over, provide, share, serve, teach, and direct."

Those are "doing words" as one of my long ago English teachers called them. We ordain and install elders and deacons and pastors in the church *to do something*. Our constitutional questions simply ask them whether they will do it. But, our constitution doesn't stop there. You were hoping! It asks then what the *congregation* will do. Whether you will accept those whom you call to positions of leadership; whether you will encourage them, respect them, and follow them. In other words, when they ask you *to do something*, will you do it? Or will you have more reasons than our constitution has questions for why you can't or won't.

Don't get me wrong. There is nothing wrong with questions. Sometimes they lead to better answers. But only so long as our questions are seeking answers about what it is God's word calls us to do and how we can do it. What do you think? I know what I think. I think I'm going to close with another parable.

Jesus didn't tell this one. I don't know who did. It's about four Presbyterians. Some of you know them. Their names are "Everybody, Somebody, Anybody, and Nobody."

According to the parable, there was an important job to be done at church. The parable doesn't say what. It could be teaching a class or serving a meal or stuffing envelopes or being on a committee or being involved in mission or serving on a board or giving more money for some special project or the operating budget. It could be remembering the church in your will. Many of us do those things generously.

But in the parable, it said, "Everybody was asked to help. Everybody was sure Somebody would. Somebody got mad because it was Everybody's job. Everybody thought Anybody could do it. But Nobody realized that Everybody wouldn't. And in the end, Everybody blamed Somebody when Nobody did what Anybody could have done."

Think! What *do* you think? What's Jesus asking of you? Are you the first son or the second son?

The Bible doesn't tell us what *they* said to Jesus then. That's because the only important answer is what you say to Jesus now.

---

1. http://www-03.ibm.com/ibm/history/exhibits/attic2/attic 2_207.html.

2. *The Constitution, Presbyterian Church (USA)*, Part II, *Book of Order*, 14.0207.09.

Parable 10

Did You Hear What Jesus Said?

Matthew 21:33-46

Did you hear what Jesus said?

The people to whom he told the parable heard him. They heard what he said. And they didn't like what they heard! It says that after they heard it, they looked for a way to arrest him and only his celebrity status stopped them.

So maybe we ought to listen again.

> *Jesus told the chief priests and leaders to listen to this story: A land owner once planted a vineyard. He built a wall around it and dug a pit to crush the grapes in. He also built a lookout tower. Then he rented out his vineyard and left the country.*
>
> *When it was harvest time, the owner sent some servants to get his share of the grapes. But the renters grabbed those servants. They beat up one, killed one, and stoned one of them to death. He then sent more servants than he did the first time. But the renters treated them in the same way.*
>
> *Finally, the owner sent his own son to the renters, because he thought they would respect him. But when they saw the man's son, they said, "Someday he will own the vineyard. Let's kill him! Then we can have it all for ourselves." So they grabbed him, threw him out of the vineyard, and killed him.*
>
> *Jesus asked, "When the owner of that vineyard comes, what do you suppose he will do to those renters?"*

The chief priests and leaders answered, "He will kill them in some horrible way. Then he will rent out his vineyard to people who will give him his share of grapes at harvest time."

Jesus replied, "You surely know that the Scriptures say, 'The stone that the builders tossed aside is now the most important stone of all. This is something the Lord has done, and it is amazing to us.' I tell you that God's kingdom will be taken from you and given to people who will do what he demands. Anyone who stumbles over this stone will be crushed, and anyone it falls on will be smashed to pieces."

When the chief priests and the Pharisees heard these stories, they knew that Jesus was talking about them. So they looked for a way to arrest Jesus. But they were afraid to, because the people thought he was a prophet.   — Matthew 21:33-46 (CEV)

Did you hear what Jesus said? Do you like it? I have a basic rule for reading scripture. If it wasn't good news you heard, you didn't hear Jesus. You heard yourself. Or you heard someone else. But you didn't hear Jesus if what you heard wasn't good.

That doesn't mean that what you hear in scripture won't be hard. Some of what Jesus says is as hard as a rock. As hard for us to hear as it was for those to whom he spoke. But the hard truth is still the truth and the truth, said Jesus, somewhere else, will make you free. The truth may be a hard thing, but it's also a good thing. And we need to hear it.

I have a little book that I've consulted over the years, titled *The Difficult Sayings of Jesus*. I got it for a dollar at a yard sale. It says:

The problem Professor Neil addresses in these thirty-four short chapters arose before the words of Jesus were ever committed to writing. Even during his ministry, what Jesus said was often misunderstood by his hearers ... Not every saying classified as "difficult" is perplexing for the same reasons. Sometimes Jesus' meaning seems clear enough ... until one tries to apply what he said to a particular case ... Some difficult sayings trouble us

76

*with their mortal rigor ... Some statements sound cal-
lous, if not actually immoral ... for the person who thinks
to fit Jesus into a theological pigeonhole, some of the
Master's words can be particularly difficult.*[1]

I look at my book whenever what Jesus has to say is difficult
for me to either accept or understand. I looked at my little book last
week. What Jesus had to say in this parable is difficult. Do you
know what William Neil said about it? Nothing! Because Jesus
didn't say what we think he said. Jesus didn't say what we would
say. *Jesus didn't say what the chief priests and leaders said! They
did.* You do. And I do. But not Jesus! Jesus didn't say what the
chief priests and leaders said in response to his story. The problem
in this parable is really our problem, because we hear ourselves,
not Jesus.

Jesus [said], "When the owner of that vineyard [in the parable]
comes, what do *you* suppose he will do to those renters?" (Matthew 21:40 CEV). "What do *you* say?" is what *Jesus* said. What
they said was, "He will kill them in some horrible way. Then he
will rent out his vineyard to people who will give him his share of
grapes at harvest time" (Matthew 21:42 CEV).

"They'll get theirs. He'll get his. They'll get what's coming to
them. He'll get what's owed to him. They'll get creamed! He'll get
revenge!" That sounds pretty much like what you and I say, or think,
or hope, when we're treated unfairly, or we're taken advantage of,
or we're cheated out of what is rightfully ours. "I don't get mad. I
get even!" Ever say that? Ever think that? Ever *do* that? Jesus didn't!
He never did and he never will. That's the gospel truth! The truth of
this parable is what it tells us about God, and what it tells us about
us. What it tells us about God is that he loves us.

I once heard Bill Moyers quote the Jewish thinker, Abraham
Joshua Heschel, who wrote: "All human history as described in the
Bible can be summarized as 'God in search of man.' "[2] God looks
for you and me because God loves you and me. God is the "hound
of heaven," as the poet Francis Thompson put it. Thompson was a
failure, and an opium addict who eventually died of tuberculosis.
He would know. God will never, ever, let us go, or leave us to our

own devices. That's the point of the parable. The picture the parable paints of God.

It's generally agreed that in the parable, the absentee owner who keeps trying is God; the murderous tenant farmers represent Israel, and in particular, its leaders (the ones who wanted to arrest Jesus); the slaves represent the prophets who have repeatedly called Israel back to faithfulness and often died for their trouble; and the "son" is Jesus himself.

One commentator notes that Matthew, in editing his gospel, actually changes the sequence of events slightly to make the parable conform to the passion narrative, the story of Jesus' death, which is prefigured by the death of the owner's son. "The parable is dominated by its allegorical interpretation," says Eugene Boring.[3]

We're supposed to make those connections, as they did. But if we do, then we must not simply accept the apparently logical and righteous answer of the chief priests and leaders as Jesus' answer, as God's answer to the question of what to do about what we do, we human beings. What we do is a matter of record. Read your Sunday paper. Turn on CNN. But what God does is not what we expect.

The twists and turns of events in the Middle East are what we have come to expect in that part of the world. But a decade or so ago, the news report was about something the people of Israel didn't expect. No one did.

The headline read, "Hardliners Cringe At Netanyahu's Embrace of Arafat." The story datelined Tel Aviv, Israel, said, "When his handshake turned into a lingering, two-handed squeeze, Israelis noticed. When he leaned over to whisper to his longtime enemy, people started talking. What was Benjamin Netanyahu doing?"[4] What was the prime minister of Israel doing, cozying up to the head of the PLO?

Netanyahu said he was looking to "negotiate peace without violence."[5] In a part of the world that's never known that, even in Jesus' day, that's a novel idea. *It's Jesus' idea!* And it was as politically difficult for Jesus as it was for the prime minister. But the parable is clear. God's answer to violence is not more violence, but more love.

78

The chief priests and leaders condemned themselves by their answer to Jesus' question. But God condemned no one! On the contrary, God died a condemned criminal, rather than condemn those who, as Jesus says in Luke's gospel, "... don't know what they're doing" (Luke 23:34-35 CEV). Those who don't get it, like the chief priests and leaders often get it wrong, like you and me.

"God forgives even those who kill his son." That's God's answer to Jesus' question. Would I do that? *Could* I do that? I don't know. I doubt it. But God can, and God does. God did, and still does, in Jesus Christ. In not doing what the chief priests and leaders said he had every right to do, could be expected to do, by our sense of justice, ought to do, God said three little words that changed the world: *I love you.*

Don't get me wrong. That doesn't mean that no one is responsible for anything, or that anything goes. "The stone that the builders tossed aside is now the most important stone of all," Jesus went on to say. "Anyone who stumbles over this stone will be crushed, and anyone it falls on will be smashed to pieces" (Matthew 21:42, 44 CEV). The gospel can be hard, because it not only tells us about God. It also tells us something about you and me, and our propensity for doing ourselves in. For stumbling over the truth.

Those who heard Jesus' parable did just that. They heard the truth of it. They responded with a "just" end to it. And only then realized that their condemnation was of themselves. The truth about themselves was a stone wall against which they bloodied their own heads.

The truth weighs as heavily as a rock on the life of one who lives a lie. Truth weighs on one for the lies we tell each other, and maybe most heavily, for the lies we tell ourselves. Jesus' parable was not told to have us condemn ourselves, but rather to have us listen to ourselves, and to each other. The parable calls us to quit living the lies — and start living the lives God intends for you and me. The gospel calls us to find peace with God in Jesus Christ, and to make peace with each other in everything we say or do.

Did you hear what Jesus said? I hope so. He said, "I love you."

1. William Neil, *The Difficult Sayings of Jesus* (Grand Rapids, Michigan: William B. Eerdmans Publishing Co., 1977), pp. vii-viii.

2. Bill Moyers, "Call and Promise," from G*enesis, A Living Conversation* (New York: Doubleday, 1996).

3. *The New Interpreter's Bible, Matthew*, Vol. 7 (Nashville: Abingdon Press, 1995), p. 414.

4. *The Lima News*, Lima, Ohio, Friday, October 4, 1996, A6.

5. *Ibid.*

Parable 11

Party Time

Matthew 22:1-14

What kind of story was that? The one Jesus told about the wedding reception? It's certainly not a bedtime story! Nor is it what we expect when we think of a "Bible story."

When I select hymns for Sunday morning I consult the "Index of Scriptural Allusions" at the back of our hymn book. Many hymns are based directly on scripture texts and the index is usually a good place to start to find hymns that reflect the lessons and the sermon. According to the "Index" out of 600 hymns there is not one in our book that even "alludes" to Jesus' story about the wedding reception. But there it is — in the Bible — in the mouth of Jesus, says Matthew. A story, a parable, about a guy who threw a big party. A wedding party — to which none of the invited guests came.

They fluffed it off and went to work instead. They tore up their invitations, and terrorized those who delivered them — finally killing them! The guy throwing the party ended up slaughtering his intended guests and burning down their town. Then he invited strangers off the street to come to his party. But one of the street people forgot his tuxedo and got bounced on his ear, back into the gutter. And Jesus said the kingdom of heaven is like that! Oh, yeah? What kind of heaven is that? What kind of story is that?

At one point last week, after I'd read it for the fiftieth time, asking exactly those questions, I found myself wondering about the food. The banquet was ready. No one came. So the food sat there, unrefrigerated, while the king did in his recalcitrant guests, and burned down the town ... and *then* they partied? Sounds like a recipe for food poisoning to me. Clearly you can't take the story "literally." So how *should* we take it? Another take on the story is found in Luke's gospel. In his translation of the New Testament, Eugene Peterson calls Luke's version, "The Story of the Dinner Party."

> *That triggered a response from one of the guests: "How fortunate the one who gets to eat dinner in God's kingdom!" Jesus followed up, "Yes. For there was once a man who threw a great dinner party and invited many. When it was time for dinner, he sent out his servants to the invited guests, saying, 'Come on in; the food's on the table.'*
>
> *"Then they all beg off, one after another making excuses. The first said, 'I bought a piece of property and need to look it over. Send my regrets.' And yet another said, 'I just got married and need to get home to my wife.'*
>
> *"The servant went back and told the master what had happened. He was outraged and told the servant, 'Quickly, get out into the city streets and alleys. Collect all who look like they need a square meal, all the misfits and homeless and wretched you can lay your hands on, and bring them here.'*
>
> *"The servant reported back, 'Master, I did what you commanded — and there's still room.' The master said, 'Then go to the country roads. Whoever you find, drag them in. I want my house full! Let me tell you not one of the originally invited is going to get so much as a bite at my dinner party.' "*
>
> — Luke 14:15-24 (The Message)

Without the violence and the vengeance, Luke's version of the story is easier to hear (and, perhaps, to understand). The invited guests who didn't come, after saying they would, were those who refused to hear Jesus' message and heed his words. Luke's story was told to "lawyers and Pharisees" (Luke 14:13), leaders in the Jewish community who rejected Jesus and his teaching. They got the message clearly. If they would not respond, said the story, others would, including "others" they would have nothing to do with. "The poor, the crippled, the lame, and the blind" (Luke 14:13). The hungry, the misfits, the homeless, the wretched.

At a time when people were considered to be poor, crippled, lame, or blind, or down on their luck because of their sins, Jesus said they were precisely the people who would be in the kingdom of heaven, instead of those who considered themselves worthy and without sin, and holding an engraved invitation.

Jesus told this story to the Jews. As Christians, listening to the story from our perspective, we have to be careful. It sounds like in accepting us (the unacceptable people in the parable), God rejected the Jews. It doesn't say that. It doesn't mean that. It's saying that in Jesus, God accepted us, but that the Jews rejected Jesus. Luke's version of the story clearly intends to say that the Jews rejected Jesus. It does *not* intend to say, however, and does *not* say that God rejected the Jews and his covenant with them, in the making of a new covenant with us all in Jesus Christ. We Christians have ignored that, misunderstood that, and forgotten that too often, and to our shame.

God has chosen to reach outside the "chosen people" to choose *all people* in Jesus Christ; that God claims us all as his children, even when we refuse to claim each other as brothers and sisters.

That said, there's still Matthew. There's still Matthew's version of the story. It would be easier to stick with Luke's version. God loves everybody, and those who exclude anybody end up excluding themselves. That's the gist of it. You could stop there. Matthew, however, with an eye to that new thing we call the church, goes further.

Matthew's version of the story is spoken not so much to the Jewish community as to the Christian community. A mixed community at that time of Jews and non-Jews alike. Commentators I consulted agree that Matthew has taken a parable directed at Jews, and recast it as an allegory directed at Christians. The gospels have agendas; you and I are Matthew's agenda.

He recasts the party as a wedding banquet. In the "Statement on the Gift of Marriage," which I read at weddings, it says, in part,

"God gave us marriage as a holy mystery in which a man and a woman are joined together, *and become one, just as Christ is one with the church.*"[1] By making the party a wedding reception, Matthew is evoking the intimate relationship between Christ and his church — saying that it's like a marriage.

The slaves sent out with invitations are first the Jewish prophets and then the Christian preachers, both of whose messages were rejected by the Jews. The destruction of "their city," in Matthew's version, is likely Matthew's own view of the actual destruction of the city of Jerusalem in the year 70, "understood" says one writer "[by Matthew] as a judgment on rebellious Israel, who had rejected the Messiah" (Matthew 4:18).[2] The servants sent out "to invite everyone ... to the wedding banquet ... both good and bad" (Matthew 22:9-10), are early Christian missionaries through whose work the new church grew beyond its Jewish roots.

So far, Matthew's story is a more forceful version of Luke's story: God loves everybody, and those who exclude anybody end up excluding only themselves. That's the way it is in the kingdom of heaven.

But now Matthew turns to the church. Matthew "will not let the audience bask complacently in the judgment pronounced on others,"[3] says one writer. It isn't just Jews who reject Jesus. It isn't just Jews who reject a word from God they don't want to hear. It's all of us. Even us Christians. Even charter members of First Church Jerusalem (and every church since)!

Matthew says, "When the king came in to see the [newly invited] guests, he noticed a man there who was not wearing a wedding robe" (Matthew 22:11). That doesn't mean the invitation said, "Black tie" and he showed up in blue jeans. The wedding attire, the "wedding robe," is a symbol for what it means to "put on Christ." To become "Christlike." To be a Christian; to be one of those invited from the streets of life to the party of a lifetime in the kingdom of God.

Paul uses the image of being "clothed," in Christ, properly attired for the party, in his letter to the Galatian church. Paul wrote, as Matthew wrote, *to Christians*, "In Christ Jesus you are all children of God through faith. As many of you as were baptized into

Christ have clothed yourselves with Christ" (Galatians 3:26-27). You have put on Christ like a piece of clothing. The cliché "clothes make the man," takes on a whole new meaning in this context.

I once attended a baptism in the Orthodox church. I always wanted to do one of those. They undressed and then dunked the naked infant, three times.

- In the name of the Father.
- In the name of the Son.
- In the name of the Holy Spirit.

And then they "clothed" the naked, dripping infant in a white robe that was not only warm and fluffy, but symbolic of being "clothed with Christ."

But Matthew wasn't being cute and cuddly with his fellow Christians. Matthew was being blunt, saying to his fellow Christians, his fellow church members, people, some of you aren't dressed properly for this party! You call yourselves Christians, but you haven't put on Christ.

This is the point where the preacher wishes he knew what the problem was at First Church Jerusalem. Matthew doesn't say. But clearly within the church there was division, dispute, or disagreement. And it must've been quite a debacle, because Matthew says the king said, "To hell with you!" — "Go to hell" are strong words for Matthew to put in the mouth of Jesus! "The king said to the attendants, 'Bind him hand and foot, and throw him into the outer darkness where there will be weeping and gnashing of teeth' " (Matthew 22:13).

Why? In the parable, because he wasn't properly dressed. In the church, because they weren't behaving properly. In their dealings with others, they weren't behaving like Christ. They were behaving, perhaps, like the good Christian members of a church in New Orleans in the late 1950s.

The Reverend Edgar Grider writes that he was new to ministry then. Racial issues were hot, and he preached a sermon on race relations.

The sermon was well prepared — biblical, pertinent, and with just the right amount of eloquence I thought.

After the service I waited for the dramatic response — contrition, repentance, life-changing decisions, admiration. There was no response to the sermon one way or another — not even enough visible anger for me to feel that my courage had been for a purpose. People simply filed out; some smiled as they usually do, others even commented on the nice weather!

That night in the officers' meeting, upon my provocation, an elder made a point of informing me quite directly that he didn't give a damn about Jesus Christ, and that this was his church. The officers — all of them — then proceeded to take appropriate action, and my eloquent sermon resulted in an official decision "to bar Negroes from the church!"[4]

The elders had no clothes! Or if they did, they were not clothed with Christ.

There's no suggestion in the parable we read that good Christians can't disagree. That is a good thing, since we often do. There is no suggestion that creative debate is bad. That quiet acquiescence is good. But there's every suggestion, and none too subtle, that when controversy and disagreements come, in church or out, we should come to them clothed with what one hymn calls "Christlike graces."[5] We should, in all our lives, and our living, be clothed with Christ.

In the parable, says one commentator, "The Jewish leaders or people are no longer in view, only the Christian hearers/readers." As in every period of the church's history, Matthew's community is composed of "both good and bad" (Matthew 22:10). Sometimes the issue is whether the community should rid itself of the bad, pull up the weeds that have grown amid the wheat (Matthew 13:24-30, 36-43). Here there seems to be no such issue, only the effort to confront the audience with the hapless and disquieting figure of the guest without a wedding garment. "Judging others is no business of the audience; rather, they are to tend to themselves, their

86

Proper 27, Pentecost 25, Ordinary Time 32

Parable 12

What We Have Left Undone

Matthew 25:1-13

There is a mistake in my Bible. Actually, I found two mistakes in the gospel reading this week. One in the text of my study Bible. The other in the action, or *inaction* of the foolish bridesmaids in Jesus' story.

The mistake I found in my study Bible was in that same story. In my leather-bound, New Oxford Annotated Bible — the one I use for study, Matthew 25:11-13 reads this way:

> *Later the other bridesmaids came also, saying, "Lord, lord, open to us." But he replied, "Truly I tell you, I do not know you." Keep awake therefore, for you know neither the day nor the hour.*[1]

You don't have to be a Bible scholar to know that someone wasn't awake when they proofread that page. Jesus' parable of the wise and foolish maidens is a wake-up call for you and me to proofread our lives.

When I was a child we used to follow Ann Landers' advice column. Some of you are old enough to remember her. Sometimes she would tell a reader to "Wake up and smell the coffee!" — to pay attention to some reality right in front of them. Jesus, in this little story, is saying the same to you and me. He is saying that reality is "no one lives forever" — so wake up and look at the way you live.

One way to look at it is that this is "the first day of the rest of your life." That sells well on card shop cards — and that's true. Another way, though, is that this could be "the last day of the rest of your life." Either way, how's your life? In the living of it, be honest now, are you wise, or are you foolish in the way you spend your days? Are you like the five wise bridesmaids who made provision, or like the five foolish bridesmaids who made a mistake?

You don't have to be an expert on Palestinian wedding customs to get the intent of the story. But it may help to put it in more modern terms. Suppose you've been asked to be a bridesmaid or a groomsman in a big fancy wedding. Appointments have been scheduled months in advance with the fitters for your dress or your tuxedo. You know when the wedding is. You know how long it takes to get your outfit ready. The bride has given you a schedule. If you're wise you don't wait 'til the last minute and you get properly dressed for the occasion. If you are foolish, you wait 'til the day before, and show up at the wedding in blue jeans. Imagine how the bride and groom will respond. That's the gist of Jesus' story. He's saying, life doesn't wait for you. As the television insurance commercial once put it: "Life comes at you fast." You have to be ready for it. Life isn't a (dress) rehearsal. It's the real thing.[2]

How's life? How are you spending your life? How's your stewardship of what God has given you?

Kristen Groetsch writes:

> Say "stewardship" in front of a church full of worshipers and they will hear, 'money!' Christian stewardship encompasses how we manage every detail of our lives and the earth itself, acknowledging all as God's gift. But the word always seems to evoke visions of pledge cards dancing in our heads.[3]

That's from an article aptly titled, "What Helps People Let Go?" I know. You just finished that sentence, "What helps people let go ... *of their money.*"

And there's no denying it. Life costs money. Lamp oil costs money. Church costs money. But cash isn't the *only* issue, nor is it even *the most important* issue when it comes to our stewardship both in church and out. Our money is really only a measure of what matters to us, and how we are spending our lives.

If you want one thing to take away to think about today, take this. Words of wisdom about the "economics" of life. Our word "economics," by the way, comes from the Greek *oikonomia* which means the management of a household. Whenever Jesus talked about a "steward" he was talking about an *oikonomos*, an "economist." Not someone who worked for the World Bank or the Federal Reserve, but someone who managed the life of a large and probably affluent household.

I have an undergraduate degree in economics and an MBA in finance. But no economist, in our sense of the word, I ever heard or read ever made more sense than the philosopher *cum* economist, Henry David Thoreau. This is what I want you to take home. Thoreau said, "The price of anything is the amount of life you exchange for it." Thoreau also put it another way: "If you give money, you spend yourself with it."[4]

That's what this little wedding story is really about. How you spend *yourself*, and whether, in the end, when midnight comes, you can say you got what you paid for. It's a *stewardship* story. It's not just, *ala* the Boy Scouts, "be prepared" lest you miss something. It's be wise in the way you spend *your life*, lest you *lose* something. Lest you lose your self.

Jesus said a lot about money because money says a lot about you and me. Jesus would agree with Thoreau. When you spend your money you spend your life. How well are you spending it?

In Jesus' story, five of the bridesmaids spent wisely; five did not. Churches do that, too. Church researcher, Michael Meier, says,

> *If your church's vision for ministry is to open the doors for worship, offer Sunday School, pay a pastor's salary and keep the lights on, then it's fine to ask the question, 'How little can we get by with?' But if your vision is to teach people the love of God and reach out to those people, then that's the wrong question.*[5]

All of us can be guilty of that — of asking the wrong question. The mistake the bridesmaids in Jesus' story made was not dozing off, but not doing what they could have done, and should have done, to get ready for the wedding because they asked the wrong question. That led to doing the wrong thing — or, actually, to not doing the right thing.

Each week, we pray together

Merciful God,
We confess that we have sinned against you
In thought, word and deed,
by what we have done,
and by what we have left undone.

Sins of *omission* (not doing the right thing) can be just as serious as sins of *commission*. Jesus was saying that in this little story, if nothing else. If you want to argue that first go read the parable of the talents and the parable of the great judgment, which immediately follow the parable of the wise and foolish bridesmaids, in the same chapter of Matthew's gospel. In each of the three parables in this section of Matthew, it's what people *didn't do* that incurred God's judgment as sin.

The mistake the foolish bridesmaids made — the sin they committed — was not doing what they should have done and what they could have done. Instead of asking the right question: "What do I need to do to get ready for this wedding?" They asked the wrong question: "What can I do to cut my costs for lamp oil?" Instead of, "How important will it be to have a good flashlight tonight?" They asked, "How can I save on batteries today?" A big mistake, as they would soon find out. It was a mistake, not because there's anything wrong with saving money; so long as "saving" money doesn't really mean "serving" money — something Jesus said often.

Serving money doesn't mean putting it on the mantle and singing hymns to it. Serving money means making *making* money and *keeping* money more important than *using* money to make things happen.

Someone sent me a cartoon from *The New Yorker* magazine. It shows a dejected man at the gates of heaven. Saint Peter is sitting at a desk and checking out the books on his life — his personal "bottom line." Saint Peter is saying to him: "You had more money than God. That's a big no-no." The note that came with the cartoon suggested it would make a good stewardship theme at church some year. You have more money than God. That's a big no-no! Let the stewardship committee tell you what to do about it.

That is not a bad idea, but I decided it wouldn't work. God doesn't have *any* money. Which means we all have more money than God has. I checked. There is no line in our church's income budget for God's giving. Only yours and mine. That's all the money God has.

Martin Luther wrote, "If God has given you wealth, give thanks to God, and see that you make the right use of it."[6] Ask the right questions. Do the right things. Spend it — *spend yourself* — wisely.

Why don't we? In church and out, we don't. Like the bridesmaids we all know what needs doing. Why don't all of us do it? Why don't we spend our days and our dollars more wisely than we do? And if we did, what would that look like? You'll have to answer that one for yourself.

The Reverend Joan Gray, moderator of the General Assembly of the Presbyterian Church, is going around saying we need to answer that one. In a speech at Massanetta Springs, Virginia, Reverend Gray said,

> *Among our leaders, [in our church] there is too much "money in the bank" thinking. If the early church had thought that way, we wouldn't be here today. As long as we stand on our "money in the bank," we'll never know what God can do.*[7]

I would add, and we'll never know what we could have done or what could have been.

The moderator is not calling for financial irresponsibility — either personally or in the church. She is asking the richest Christians the world has ever known to look ahead like wise bridesmaids and invest *ourselves*, days and dollars, in the coming kingdom of God. To realize what we could do *and do it*.

I found another story about that. Jesus liked stories. He could have told this one. It's titled, "Just What Could We Do?"

93

The treasurer of a congregation resigned. [I can't imagine why?] The church asked another person to take his position, a man who managed the local grain elevator. The man agreed, under two conditions: 1) That no reports from the treasurer be given for one full year; and 2) That no one ask him any questions during this one-year period.

The church board members gulped, but finally agreed. He was a trusted man in the community and well known since most of them did business with him as manager of the local grain elevator. He was a wealthy man who clearly understood how to handle money. He handled their money every day. He could handle God's money, too.

A year passed. At the meeting of the congregation to review the previous year the treasurer had this report to make. The $250,000 the church owed the bank had been paid off. The minister's salary had been increased substantially. Mission giving was up dramatically. Long deferred maintenance on the church building had been completed. There were no outstanding bills. And the balance in the checking account was more than next year's budget.

A shocked congregation asked "How come?" How could that be possible — suspecting that perhaps their wealthy treasurer had done it for them himself. "No, *you did it*!" he said quietly. "Most of you bring your grain to my elevator. As you did business with me, for the past year, I simply withheld ten percent on your behalf and gave it to the church in your name. You never missed it. Do you see what we *could* do if we would do what we could?"

You know what strikes me as most sad about those foolish bridesmaids? That money wasn't the problem. They weren't short on cash. It says so. When they finally realized what was happening, they rushed off to a first-century CVS, an all-night drugstore, to buy oil for their lamps — batteries for their lights. They had the money! But by the time they got back it was too late. Too late for what? In the story, the wedding. But Jesus said it has something to do with the kingdom of God.

I don't read this as some do, as a threat that you'd better get your act together in this life, lest it be too late and you miss the good stuff in the next. I read it differently. This is the life you have.

94

Don't miss this one! Spend it wisely. God will take care of the next.

So what did you confess this morning? Those things you've "left undone"? There's still time to do them!

---

1. *The New Oxford Annotated Bible* (Nashville: Abingdon Press, 1995), 38NT.

2. Attributed to Australian businessman, Kerry Packer.

3. Kristen Groetsch, "What Helps People Let Go?" *The Lutheran*, September 1996.

4. Source unknown.

5. *Op cit*, Groetsch.

6. *Ibid.*

7. http://www.rocktownweekly.com/news_details.hp?AID=5618&CHID=2.

Parable 13

Faith Like Fanny's

Matthew 25:14-30

I have a little book titled, *You Are What You Believe* in my library. In today's world, where belief translates so easily into violence, that title says more, I think, than John Killinger had in mind when he wrote his little book by that title on the "Apostles' Creed."

"You are what you believe." That thought helped me focus this week on the meaning of Jesus' parable about the three men entrusted by their master with with the responsibility of managing his money. I don't like this parable. I know Jesus told it, but I still don't like it. I don't like it because I want to empathize with the fall guy in the story. The guy who takes a fall in the end for doing what was arguably the best he could. In the end, he is dubbed "worthless" and fit for nothing but to be thrown out. Not just fired for not doing his job, but told, effectively, by his boss to go to hell — literally.

"As for this worthless slave [said the boss] throw him into the outer darkness, where there will be weeping and gnashing of teeth" (Matthew 25:30). For what? For playing it safe? Eugene Peterson interprets it that way in his translation of the Bible: "Get rid of this 'play-it-safe' who won't go out on a limb. Throw him out into utter darkness" (Matthew 25:30 The Message).

J. B. Phillips translates: "Throw this useless servant into the darkness outside, where he can weep and wail over his stupidity."[1] He's a worthless, useless, stupid, play-it-safe, who deserves to be damned for failing to be as good a portfolio manager as the other two men in the story.

I was fired once. Maybe that's why I empathize. But I got a severance package, a going away lunch, and the concern and support of colleagues who believed I was being scapegoated. (If you're curious, ask me, and I'll tell you the story sometime.)

I read Jesus' story every which way but upside down this week trying to make sense out of the master's judgment: "You wicked and lazy slave" (Matthew 25:26a). Strong words! It's possible, I suppose, that the man believed that about himself. And, perhaps, in believing that became that. If Killinger is right, and you *are* what you *believe*, maybe it was true. Maybe that's why, when the other two were proudly announcing their success, he was admitting his fear. He said, "Master, I knew that you were a harsh man, reaping where you did not sow, and gathering where you did not scatter seed; so I was afraid" (Matthew 25:24-25).

The curious thing is that until we get to the master's reaction there is no indication in the story that there was anything to be afraid of. On the contrary, the master had entrusted each of the men with a large amount of money to manage on his behalf.

Our word "talent" came into English because of the wide circulation of this story. But in this story a "talent" is not what will make you an "American Idol"; it's money. A talent was the equivalent of fifteen years of wages for a common laborer. In our terms, at $10 per hour for forty hours a week, the man who got five talents got the equivalent of $1,560,000 to manage. The man who got two, got about $600,000. The man who got one, about $300,000. The master clearly had differing assessments of each man's ability, but he trusted all three men. He had faith in each of them. He believed in them.

As each of the first two men made their financial report the master's response was the same: "Well done, good and trustworthy slave; you have been trustworthy in a few things, I will put you in charge of many things; enter into the joy of your master" (Matthew 25:21, 23). His joy was short-lived, however. There was no more "mister-nice-guy" when the third slave came and handed over only what he had been handed some time before; having done nothing with it.

"A parable has been defined as 'an earthly story with a heavenly meaning.' "[2]

C. H. Dodd wrote:

> *At its simplest the parable is a metaphor or a simile drawn from nature or common life, arresting the hearer by its vividness or strangeness, and leaving the mind in sufficient doubt about its precise application to tease it into active thought.*[3]

I was "teased" this week to wonder what Jesus' point was in painting this picture of this pitiful man, and saying: "the kingdom of heaven will be like this" (Matthew 25:1).

The key is to remember *it is a parable.* It's not "true." But within it lies a great "truth." It never happened, but it happens all the time. A parable is a pointed way of making a point about the hearer.

You're *supposed* to do what I did, to be teased into identifying yourself with the protagonist. And in the process, identifying in him the truth — about you. Parables have a way of making people who really pay attention to them uncomfortable. Parables got Jesus killed. People kept finding themselves in them and not liking what they found.

Willilam Barclay writes:

> *The parables were weapons of controversy, struck off in the heat of the moment ... The parable is essentially a sword to stab men's minds awake ... It must be that one single truth the story illuminates which leaps out to meet the listener's mind.*[4]

What leaps to mind for you in Jesus' story? That's the sermon this morning, and only you can write it, preach it, with your life.

This little story really has three audiences. The Jews to whom Jesus told it. The early church for which Matthew recorded it. And you and me.

99

Barclay wrote that the man who buried his talent,

> *... undoubtedly ... stands [first] for the Scribes and Pharisees and the orthodox Jews [to whom Jesus told it]. Their one aim in life was to keep things as they were. They said themselves that all they wanted was to build a fence around the law. That is why they crucified Jesus. He came with new ideas about God, about life and about a man's duty in life; and because they would have nothing to do with new ideas they crucified him.*[5]

Jesus challenged those who believed only in preserving the past, or their position in the present, at the expense of the future. He "stab[bed] men's minds awake,"[6] with little stories. They stabbed him in his side with a spear.

A second audience for this story is indicated by Matthew in his recording of it in his gospel. Scholars agree it was Matthew who gives the story its biblical context as a descriptor for the kingdom of heaven. Matthew's mission was to speak the truth to a church that had to learn to live with the already but not yet. With the promise of Jesus to be with them and the apparent absence of Jesus from them.

In that absence, that interim time before Jesus' return, Matthew tells them how to live. He told them to live like the man who had five talents, and the man who had two, making something of yourself, using God's gifts — believing in yourself because God believes in you. Don't live like the man who, in refusing risk, refused the faith his master had in him and risked his own life. The man who in burying his talent buried himself.

In the early church, Christians practiced their faith at great risk to themselves and those they loved. This parable, which in Matthew's view casts Jesus as the master, ascended to heaven, from which he is yet to return, to demand an accounting, sounded a warning to early Christians not to slack off and just hold on and wait. But as an old hymn I grew up singing says, I can hear Matthew saying:

> *We'll work till Jesus comes*
> *And we'll be gathered home.*[7]

The moral of the tale, according to Matthew, is make use of the gifts God has given you to serve him, until you see him coming and it is finally on earth as it is in heaven.

And then there's you and me. We're an audience for this story, too. What does the parable say to you? Let me suggest that at least it should hold you accountable — me, too — for those sins of omission we confessed earlier. Those things we *didn't* do. The man with one talent didn't do anything wrong. He just didn't do anything. And *that* was wrong.

We prayed:

> *Merciful God,*
> *We confess that we have sinned against you*
> *In thought, word and deed,*
> *by what we have done,*
> and by what we have left undone.

Often as not, it's the sin of *not doing* that undoes us. It isn't the awful things we've done, but the good things not done, that do us in.[8]

Barclay makes several points that are particularly relevant to you and me. First, Barclay writes, we have *different gifts*. The parable underscores that. God knows that. The man who did nothing wasn't asked to do everything. He was asked to do what, in the master's estimation, he *could* do: manage one talent. Says Barclay,

> *We are all born with different abilities and the test is how we use the abilities we have ... The whole duty of life is not to envy someone else his skill but to make the best of our own ... The ultimate aim in life must be to say in all sincerity, "I have done my best."*[9]

Second, "This parable condemns the man who will not try." I'm convinced that if the man had tried and failed — lost the talent — the master's response to him would have been as it was for the others: "Enter into the joy of your master." The sin was not not succeeding, but not trying.

Barclay observes:

> ... *Very likely the unworthy servant felt that it was not worth trying. He had only one talent and it did not seem worthwhile trying to use it. But the world is not composed of geniuses. For the most part it is composed of ordinary people doing ordinary jobs, but these ordinary jobs must be done if the world is to go on and God's plans worked out. It has been said with great wisdom, "God does not want extraordinary people who do extraordinary things nearly so much as he wants ordinary people who do ordinary things extraordinarily well" ... The world depends on the man with the one talent.*[10]

And finally, Barclay again, "This parable lays it down that what we do not use we are bound in the end to lose."[11]

That's certainly true of our "talents" in the biblical sense — our money. No one yet has managed to do other than leave it behind in the end. Someone once said, what you get is a living, what you give is a life. "Use it or lose it." Sixteenth-century English composer, Thomas Ravenscroft, is remembered best not for his music but for his insight which appears in varying forms. Ravenscroft said, "What I gave I have; what I spent I had; what I left I lost by not giving it."[12]

And that's true in every aspect of life, from sports, to relationships to faith. If you don't practice, don't expect to play well. If you don't relate, relationships die. If you don't remain faithful, your faith will go to hell.

Fanny Bell did well, I think, with all those. Fanny, who died this past week at 98, was a member of my Ohio congregation. Fanny was a Scot. She never forgave me for not playing golf. Fanny practiced golf. Fanny won golf tournaments. Fanny played until she couldn't see the ball! In her mid nineties Fanny was still at church every week helping put the weekly church newsletter together for mailing. It was a time when she and her friends talked and laughed and ate donuts — and also did some work that needed doing.

102

Every year, Fanny went to Arizona to visit her daughter "for the last time." I lost count of how many times she did that. Fanny's "onions" were legendary at church potlucks, and her Scottish shortbread was a Christmas gift to be savored. Fanny gave friendship and got friends in return. Fanny's faith was as deep as any I've ever seen. I don't mean we always agreed on every point of Christian doctrine. We didn't, but she lived what she believed. She was faithful to her God to the end. Into her nineties Fanny would share her faith with children at church programs, teaching and touching lives as she could. She shared her faith with me.

Fanny's gone now. I said good-bye to her a few years ago at her funeral. There was little Fanny left undone and a lot she left behind for those who knew her. For me Fanny was the proof of it. You *are* what you believe. Believe that God believes in you!

Afterword

After I preached this sermon one of my members sent me an email that said in part:

> *Your sermon last week ... struck a chord. It reminded me of one of my favorite poems from my childhood ... my sister had to memorize the entire poem for a choral speaking group at our church. At the time I was too young to join, but I went with her to the rehearsals and ended up learning bits and pieces of the things they rehearsed. I have always loved this poem because they are truly words to live by. It is a gentle reminder that it is the cumulative effect of daily kindnesses that enriches our lives and that of those around us. Grace, joy and a positive attitude are catching!*

The poem goes as follows:

> *It isn't the thing you do, dear,*
> *It's the thing you leave undone*
> *That gives you a bit of a heartache*
> *At setting of the sun.*

The tender word forgotten,
The letter you did not write,
The flowers you did not send, dear,
Are your haunting ghosts at night.

The stone you might have lifted
Out of a brother's way;
The bit of heartsome counsel
You were hurried too much to say;
The loving touch of the hand, dear,
The gentle, winning tone
Which you had no time nor thought for
With troubles enough of your own.

Those little acts of kindness
So easily out of mind,
Those chances to be angels
Which we poor mortals find —
They come in night and silence,
Each sad, reproachful wraith,
When hope is faint and flagging,
And a chill has fallen on faith.

For life is all too short, dear,
And sorrow is all too great,
To suffer our slow compassion
That tarries until too late:
And it isn't the thing you do, dear,
It's the thing you leave undone
Which gives you a bit of heartache
At the setting of the sun.

— Margaret Sangster 1838-1912[13]

---

1. J. B. Phillips, *The New Testament in Modern English* (New York: The Macmillan Company, 1964), p. 57. Used by permission. This is a Macmillan Inc. title, now under the control of Simon & Schuster, www.simonsays.com, Yessenia. Santos@simonandschuster.com, Permissions Department.

2. William Barclay, *The Parables of Jesus* (Louisville: Westminster John Knox Press, 1970), p. 12.

3. C. H. Dodd, *The Parables of the Kingdom* (New York: Harper and Row, 1981), p. 5.

4. *Op cit*, Barclay, p. 16.

5. *Ibid*, 169.

6. *Ibid*, 16.

7. Elizabeth Kay Mills, "O Land Of Rest, For Thee I Sigh!"

8. After this sermon was preached a member of my congregation sent me a copy of a poem called "The Sin of Omission," by Margaret E. Sangster. It is reprinted on pages 105-106.

9. *Op cit*, William Barclay, pp. 171-172.

10. *Ibid*, p. 172.

11. *Ibid*.

12. www.brainyquote.com.

13. Margaret E. Sangster, "The Sin of Omission," *The Home Book of Verse: American and English 1580-1920*, ed. Burton Egbert Stevenson, 5th edn. (New York: Henry Holt, 1922), pp. 2926-2927.

Christ The King, Proper 29

Parable 14

Narrow Love?

Matthew 25:31-46

Okay — I confess. I watched the closing minutes of the finale of *America's Got Talent* in 2006. The show is a cross between *The Ed Sullivan Show* and *The Gong Show*. If you're too young to remember any of that, never mind!

In an attempt to heighten the suspense, host Regis Philbin had the eight or ten finalists come out on the stage, proceeded to divide them into two equal groups, made them sit in chairs on opposite sides of the stage, wait through a commercial break, and then declared one group potential winners, and the other group losers.

The panel of judges tried to mute the moment and make everyone feel good by declaring everyone who made it that far "winners," but everyone knew that only one of them would win a million dollars. I chuckled when the million dollar winner, who not long before was belting out songs and being compared with Liza Minelli was so shocked by winning that Regis couldn't coax her to say a thing. All that hype came down to the blank, teary-eyed face of a little girl who suddenly looked very "eleven," and whose silence spoke volumes as Regis kept saying, "You all right? Bianca, how do you feel, darling? You okay?"[1]

Football coach, Vince Lombardi, is credited with saying that, "Winning isn't everything, it's the *only* thing." I wonder. Do you have to "win" to be okay? Does "winning" *make* you okay? What about the "runners-up"?

The harmonica player won an automobile. Did he "win"? Does that count? And what about those people on the other side of the

107

stage? They had to "win" to get there, but in the end what did they get? In vaudeville terms, they got "the hook." They had to leave the stage to the "winners."

I know a lot of life is like that. But is that really what Jesus wanted to tell us in the story I read? That the kingdom of heaven is like that, too? Winners and losers? Winners take all; losers take a hike? The prize is "heaven"? The "booby prize" is "hell"?

I looked up "booby prize." It's literally the "idiot's prize." In Spanish, the *premio de consolación*. The consolation prize. But is there really any consolation in *losing*? I'm asking more questions than I'm answering. The "parable" of the sheep and the goats does that, too — raises more questions than it answers.

Over the years, when I've run into such questions in preaching I've consulted a little book titled *The Difficult Sayings of Jesus* by William Neil. The Reverend Doctor Neil is a Scot. So he would appreciate the fact that I bought his little book at a yard sale for $1. Or maybe he wouldn't! In any event I consulted him this week. His book has 34 chapters covering 34 difficult sayings of Jesus. But not a word about the sheep and goats — about sheep who find themselves in the care of a loving shepherd. That's a big "win" if there ever was one. And what about goats who go to hell? Losers do, you know, or do they? I'm not sure if Neil thought that was easy — or decided it was too hard to handle.

The simple, commonly accepted interpretation of this story is summarized well by another Scot, the theologian, William Barclay.

> This is one of the most vivid parables Jesus ever spoke, and the lesson is crystal clear — that God will judge us in accordance with *our reaction to human need. His judgment does not depend on the knowledge we have amassed, or the fame that we have acquired, or the fortune that we have gained, but on* the help that we have given ... *God will judge us in accordance with ... the help that we have given.*[2]

Well, won't he?

Douglas Hare, writing in his commentary on Matthew's gospel says:

> *It is customary to interpret this passage in universal terms: at the last judgment all will be judged on the basis of how they have treated the needy and distressed. This understanding has inspired generations of Christians to pay closer attention to their sins of omission instead of concentrating exclusively on sins of commission (adultery, dishonesty, bad temper, lying, etc.)* This passage reminds us that what we don't do also gets us into trouble.[3]

Our prayer of confession says,

> *Merciful God,*
> *we confess that we have sinned against you*
> *in thought, word and deed,*
> *by what we have done,*
> and by what we have left undone.

And so we have sinned against God — both ways, "by what we have done *and* by what we have left undone."

I grew up in a form of Christianity that seemed to define faith with one word: "Don't!" In this passage Jesus seems to define it differently: "Do!" Not only that, but *don't* "do" and God help you!

My wife has a coffee mug, actually for her it's a tea mug, that I think she got from my former church secretary. On the side it says, "Damned if you do, Damned if you don't." Is that the gospel? Is that "good news"? Do we really need God to tell us that or could we figure that out for ourselves? Surely I am not the only person in the room for whom that is sometimes true — "No matter what I do ... da-da, da-da, da-da." Does that mean that I "baa," or that I "bleat"? Does it mean that I am a sheep, or I am a goat, in the eyes of God?

In the Bible, "sheep" are those needing tending by a shepherd. And images of the "good shepherd" are found throughout. The psalmist says, "The Lord is my *shepherd*" (Psalm 23:1), not, "The Lord is my *goatherd*."

In the Jewish sacrificial rituals of Jesus day, goats carried the sins of the world, or at least the community, out into the desert where, with the goat, they died. That's where we get our term "scapegoat." The one who carries the sins, the faults, of others, away. In Leviticus God says that having sacrificed one goat as a "sin offering" (Leviticus 16:9), another goat "shall be presented alive before the Lord to make atonement over it, that it may be sent away into the wilderness to Azazel [possibly a desert demon]" (Leviticus 16:10).

> Then Aaron [who at this point in the story had taken over for Moses] shall lay both his hands on the head of the live goat, and confess over it all the iniquities of the people of Israel, and all their transgressions, all their sins, putting them on the head of the goat, and sending it away into the wilderness by means of someone designated for the task. The goat shall bear on itself all their iniquities to a barren region; and the goat shall be set free in the wilderness.   — Leviticus 16:21-22

A wilderness where, according to the Jewish *Talmud*, the goat was pushed over a cliff.

Goats get a bad deal in the Bible. What "gets my goat" is how readily you and I buy into imagery that suggests that in the end it is the same. The good get goodies, and the bad get theirs. The "bad" of course, being "them" or "those people."

But God's grace is more gracious than that. As one hymn writer puts it:

> For the love of God is broader
> Than the measures of man's mind;
> And the heart of the Eternal
> Is most wonderfully kind.[4]

Whenever you read a text like the one this morning, and the news you hear isn't "good," or isn't "kind" read it again. I did this week. Lots of times.

If I were God I can think of a good number of goats I'd run off to their destruction. But I'm not God. And I need, when reading a text like this one, to remember that the one sitting on the throne is not me. I am before the throne, not on it! One reading of this text would suggest that "all the nations ... gathered before [the throne]" aren't me either. That you and I are not in this story at all. For reasons having to do with Matthew's choice of words, and other scholarly analysis, Douglas Hare, calls this segment of Matthew, "The Judgment of the Pagans."[5]

In his commentary, Hare argues that there is good reason to believe that this story is not about everyone but specifically about the *ethne,* the Greek word translated "nations," who are, in Hebrew the *goyyim,* which at the time of Jesus meant the "Gentiles." Those not of the Jewish faith, and in Matthew's context, not the new Christians either. Hare believes this passage, if it goes back to Jesus at all, is being used by Matthew to suggest that it is possible that God just might decide to save some who are not like us.

> *A number of ancient Jewish texts express concern for "righteous Gentiles." Jews living in contact with pagans were not slow to observe that, despite their idolatry, some pagans were genuinely good people. Was it fair for them to be eternally damned?*[6]

I've had good Christians ask me privately whether their good Jewish, or good Buddhist, or good Hindu, or for that matter good *atheist* friends, were automatically damned to eternal destruction because they did not "accept Jesus Christ as their Lord and Savior." Given that some of the best people, most honest people, most generous people, most pleasant people I know are *not* Christians; and some of the worst people, most dishonest people, stingiest people, downright obnoxious people I know *are* — card carrying, baptized Christians, Hare's take on this is helpful.

The church for which Matthew was writing lived in the midst of a non-Christian world just like us. To read Paul's letters, Christians then were just like Christians now. The question of the salvation of their non-Christian neighbors was bound to come up. It's just possible that this is Matthew's answer. That God is God, and the good we do in this life may engender or reflect the grace of God in the next. That while we debate endlessly who's in and who's out, Jesus finally found it necessary to say in another setting that "God did not send the Son into the world to condemn the world but in order that the world might be saved through him" (John 3:17). "The world" in John 3 is *kosmos* — the whole of life, the whole world, all of God's creation.

God is not Regis Philbin! (And not Dick Sheffield, either.) God does not need losers to make some of us winners. God, in Jesus Christ, can make "winners" of us all. In the end, is the issue that we have "accepted Jesus Christ as our Lord and Savior," or is it that in Jesus Christ God has accepted us? This story doesn't settle that perennial Christian debate, but it ought to make us wary of settling it too quickly.

One source I read suggested that this seemingly simple, yet curiously complex, story is not actually a parable at all. A parable is an earthly story that contains within it a heavenly truth. This is a heavenly story, or, I guess, depending on your perspective, a hellish story, that contains within it an earthly truth. It matters how we treat one another. It matters how we build hells for one another; or how, by what we build, we give one another a glimpse of heaven. Whatever else this story is, it is not our "go ahead" to sit in judgment of one another. Instead, it judges you and me.

In the story the king judges between those who were guilty of what they had left undone and those favored for what they had done. But it's more subtle than that. It's more than a *quid pro quo*; something for something; good for good; evil for evil; what you need to do to win, in this life or the next. The Reformation, of which we are heirs, rejected the notion that we can "earn" our way into heaven. The most interesting feature of the story, I think, is the surprise of both groups when judgment was rendered. You can almost hear it: "Who?" "Me?" "I did?" "I didn't?"

At weddings, as part of the "Statement on the Gift of Marriage," I read: "In marriage, husband and wife are called to a new way of life, created, ordered and blessed by God. This way of life must not be entered into carelessly, or from selfish motives, but responsibly and prayerfully." What's true for marriage is true for all of life, says this story. It isn't just what we do, but why we do it. What our motives are. Whether we serve or we are just self-serving.

The story does not suggest that if the "goats" had just done more good deeds they would have been accounted "sheep." Like in the way the harmonica player could have won the other night if he had played better. But that the sheep — sheep by virtue of their living life out of the love of God — shared that love with others without expecting a reward, and were then surprised with life worth living forever.

That applies *now*, never mind later. As someone once said, "Love God and do as you please, for if you truly love God, what you do will please God."

We all know someone who lives like that. I've known many. Among them a woman named Esther Hirsch. I will always remember Esther Hirsch, and give thanks to God for people like her.

I can still see the counter in the store which she ran, along with Mr. Hirsch, in the neighborhood where I lived as a child. I can see her smile. I can hear the pride she took in kids like me in her voice. A few years ago, Esther died. Her obituary read, " 'Nickel lady' Hirsch dies at 93."

> Generations received a reward for A's brought to Esther Hirsch's store ... For every A a child earned at ... school, Hirsch would pay a nickel. All they had to do was bring their report card to Hirsch's Department Store, just a few blocks from the ... school and only a block away from the sprawling textile mill(s) where most of the folks made their living.[7]

That's where I lived. Where I went to school. I got a lot of nickels. I got good grades. I've got proof. I've got those old report cards. Mama saved them. There were six grading periods, and six classes in each, for six years of grade school. I got $10.80 in nickels from Mrs. Hirsch. I suspect she gave away thousands of dollars to thousands of children over too many years to remember. But what mattered to me was those nickels and knowing I mattered. I didn't know much about the larger world around me then. I didn't know much about Mrs. Hirsch. I just knew what she did without expecting anything from kids like me. I didn't know Mrs. Hirsch was Jewish. I didn't know that some would say she would go to hell — not for what she did, but for what she didn't do. Become a Christian like me.

Either Martin Luther or Will Rogers said, "If there is no laughter in heaven, I don't want to go there!" If people like Mrs. Hirsch aren't going to be there, I don't either. Matthew seems to be suggesting there will be.

Frederick Faber wrote, "There's A Wideness In God's Mercy," a familiar hymn that originally ended with these words we no longer sing.

> *But we make His love too narrow*
> *By false limits of our own;*
> *And we magnify His strictness*
> *With a zeal He will not own.*
>
> *Was there ever kinder shepherd*
> *Half so gentle, half so sweet,*
> *As the Savior who would have us*
> *Come and gather at His feet?*[8]

Sounds to me like a good hymn for sheep and goats to sing together.

---

1. http://www.washingtonpost.com/wp-dyn/content/article/2006/08/18/AR2006081800321.html.

2. William Barclay, *The Daily Study Bible, The Gospel of Matthew*, Volume 2 (Philadelphia: The Westminster Press, 1975), p. 325.

3. Douglas R. A. Hare, *Matthew — Interpretation, a Bible Commentary for Teaching and Preaching* (Louisville, Kentucky: Westminster John Knox Press, 1993), p. 288 (emphasis added).

4. "There's A Widness In God's Mercy," words by Frederick W. Faber, 1854; music by Lizzie S. Tourjee, 1877.

5. *Op cit*, Douglas R. A. Hare, pp. 288-291.

6. *Ibid.*

7. *The Ledger-Enquirer*, Columbus, Georgia.

8. http://www.cyberhymnal.org/htm/t/h/e/therwide.htm.

WARNING
Removing or tampering with the card on the back side of this page renders this book non-returnable.

Title: Preaching The Parables, Series IV, Cycle A

ISBN: 0-7880-2458-2

INSTRUCTIONS TO ACCESS PASSWORD FOR ELECTRONIC COPY OF THIS TITLE:

The password appears on the reverse side of this page. Carefully cut the card from the page to retrieve the password.

Once you have the password, go to

http:/www.csspub.com/passwords/

and locate this title on that web page. By clicking on the title, you will be guided to a page to enter your password, name, and email address. From there you will be sent to a page to download your electronic version of this book.

For further information, or if you don't have access to the internet, please contact CSS Publishing Company at 1-800-241-4056 in the United States (or 419-227-1818 from outside the United States) between 8 a.m. and 5 p.m., Eastern Standard Time, Monday through Friday.